NATIVE AMERICAN
PLACE NAMES
OF
MAINE,
NEW HAMPSHIRE,
& VERMONT

R. A. DOUGLAS-LITHGOW

APPLEWOOD BOOKS
Bedford, Massachusetts

*Native American Place Names of Maine, New Hampshire, &
Vermont* was published originally in 1909 as part of *Indian
Place and Proper Names of New England.*

Thank you for purchasing an Applewood Book.
Applewood reprints America's lively classics—books
from the past that are still of interest to modern readers.
For a free copy of our current catalog, please write to
Applewood Books, P.O. Box 365, Bedford, MA 01730.

ISBN 1-55709-541-8

Library of Congress Catalog Card Number: 2001086348

10 9 8 7 6 5 4 3 2 1

CONTENTS.

PREFACE

"The names which the original inhabitants assigned to our mountains, plains and valleys, are mostly lost. Many of our rivers, bays, and falls of water are yet known by their ancient Indian names. On account of their originality, antiquity, signification, singularity, and sound, these names ought to be carefully preserved. In every respect they are far preferable to the unmeaning application, and constant repetition of an improper English name.

Samuel Williams, LL.D., Natural and Civil History of Vermont.
Vol. 1, p. 43. 1809.

My sole aim in the production of this volume has been to collect the accessible Native American place and proper names of Maine, New Hampshire, and Vermont, and to give the locations of the one, with their interpretations, as far as possible, and the tribal affiliations of the other. No attempt has been made to enter into their philological significance, and where the geographical setting of orthographical varieties of the same name presents approximate but different localities, it is because I have found them so described by different authorities. I have, moreover, culled these names from every practicable source that I could discover, so that they might be preserved for those who may take an interest in them now or hereafter.

These words represent almost all that remains of the aboriginal inhabitants of this country,— a brave, noble and patriotic race who, opposed by the overwhelming and heedless forces of civilization, did everything the bravest and noblest could do to obey the first law of Nature: self-preservation. The race has almost disappeared from our New England States, and the means used for its effacement reflect little credit upon their successors; but there are many, and an increasing number, who cherish and would keep green memories of the vanquished aborigines, and I must include myself among them.

It is really marvellous that so many of the aboriginal names are spared to us especially when we remember that the Indians had no written language,—that in the north-ern New England States the French missionaries and the early settlers had to reproduce as nearly as possible the spoken word by phonetic means alone, and that through-out the more southerly States, the early English settlers had only similar means at their disposal. It is scarcely, therefore, a matter for surprise that many of the original Indian words have become more or less corrupt in their formation and orthography, and that their original char-acter has been lost by their transference from one lan-guage to another. The ignorance of scribes, and the absence of orthographical exactitude prevailing general-ly during the 17th century have made confusion more confounded, so that, in many cases, as Trumbull says, the words have "suffered some mutilation or change of form." Thanks, however, to the efforts of many scholarly men, some of whom were contemporary with the Indians, lin-guistic and dialectical difficulties have been to some extent surmounted, and in numerous instances the true character, orthographical correctness and real significa-tion of the words have been reproduced and restored.

In a few instances place-names have been intro-duced which, strictly speaking, should not have been included within the scope of this volume, but, as these names constantly recur throughout the history of New England during the 17th century it has been thought advisable to retain them.

Where several forms of the same place-name are given I have wherever practicable, indicated the forms generally accepted by having them italicised.

With regard to the place-names of Conn: I have been compelled, for obvious reasons, to make free use of the late Dr. Trumbull's classical work on this subject, but, at the same time I have materially increased the number of names. Mr. S. S. Rider's admirable work on "The Lands of Rhode Island" has been simply invaluable with regard to the place-names of this State, and I hereby gratefully express my obligation.

My cordial thanks are due to Lucius C. Hubbard, Esq., the Hon. J. G. Crawford, and Hon. S. A. Green, M. D., LL. D. for permission to select from or reproduce Indian words and place-names contained in their respective works; also to the Librarians of the several New England Historical Societies for ever-ready and highly esteemed assistance.

To the courteous Librarian of the Boston Public Library, Horace G. Wadlin, Esq., and his efficient staff, especially to Miss Agnes Doyle, and Mr. Blaisdell,— I am deeply indebted for never-failing kindness in their respective departments; and also to W. Prescott Greenlaw, Esq., Librarian of the New England Historic Genealogical Society.

To Otis G. Hammond, Esq., M. A., Assistant Editor of the State Papers, at the State Library, Concord, N. H., I owe a special debt of gratitude for valuable cooperation cordially and generously rendered; also to H. A. Wright, Esq., of Springfield, Mass., author of "Indian Deeds," an excellent work, which I have found most useful.

I have also received uniform kindness from Professor F. W. Hodge, and Professor W. H. Holmes, of Washington, D. C.; Professor Perkins of Burlington University, Vermont; Warren K. Moorehead, Esq., A. M., of Phillip's Academy (Archaeological Department), Andover, Mass.; C. C. Willoughby, Esq., Peabody Museum, Harvard University; S. S. Rider, Esq.. Providence; the Rev. Joseph Anderson, D. D., of Waterbury, Conn.; Dr. Benjamin Sharp, of Nantucket; James W. Colby, Esq., of Waltham, Mass.; W. Wallace Tooker, Esq., of Sag Harbor, N. Y. and many other correspondents to whom I now tender grateful acknowledgments.

It is by no means claimed that the lists of Place-names in this volume are exhaustive: I have, however, done my best, and any additional names forwarded to the writer will be gratefully received for future use.

My task has not been an easy one; but if the result is found to supply a want, which I know has been very frequently expressed, in the Public and State Libraries throughout the country, I shall not regret the labor I have expended.

R. A. DOUGLAS-LITHGOW.

BOSTON,
    MASS.

INTRODUCTION

THE AMERICAN–INDIANS IN NEW ENGLAND.

Long previous to the landing of the Pilgrims, at Plymouth, in December, 1620, and for at least a century afterwards, the aborigines, known as Indians, occupied the territory which is now New England, and maintained the same relative positions. It would be manifestly inappropriate here to hazard any opinion as to the original source from which this primitive people emanated, and especially so in the face of the many theories that have already been propounded as to their origin. The whole matter is still a *quæstio vexata*; but, as anthropological research has never, perhaps, been so active and persistent as at present, it is to be hoped that increasing light and knowledge may lead to the elucidation of a problem which has hitherto baffled all efforts for its solution.

The term Indian, as first applied to the American aborigines by early European travellers,— who mistook the American coast for part of Asia,— was an unqualified misnomer: but, when this ancient race was found scattered over the whole land, the same term was used to designate them wherever they were located, and they have been thus uniformly described ever since, although now distinguished as American-Indians, or Amerinds.

MAINE. The aboriginal people identified with Maine consisted of the *Abnaki*, or *Abenaqui*, a confederacy of tribes forming a sub-group of the great Algonquian Stock. The name Abnaki was first applied to the Indians in Nova Scotia, but was afterwards used to designate all the tribes who resided east of Massachusetts, and especially those who inhabited the Western part of Maine, and who frequently overflowed into the northern section of New Hampshire. The name comes from *Wabunaki*, meaning "land or country of the east," or "morning land." It has been recently estimated that they numbered about 2500 in the year 1600. They were divided into the following principal tribes:

The Sokokis or Sochigones, settled on or about the Saco river.

The Arosaguntacooks or Arsikantegou, on or about the Androscoggin river.

The Kanibas, or Norridgewocks, on or about the Kennebec river.

The Penobscots or Pentugouet, on or about the Penobscot river.

The Pequawkets or Pegouakki, in New Hampshire.

The Amaseconti or Aumissoukanti on Farmington Falls, Sandy river.

The Wewenocks or Wawenocks, east of Sagadahoc to St. George's River.

The Rocamekos, a branch of the Pequawkets, at Fryeburg.

The Etchemin tribe inhabited the eastern part of the state, extending from the Penobscot to the St. Croix river, and into New Brunswick as far as St. Johns. Although the earlier writers refer to the Etchemin as a family distinct from the Abnaki, modern anthropologists regard them as descendants of the same original stock, but differing dialectically from them. They are known also as Malecites or Maliseets, and as Passamaquoddies, as in later years, they have resided on the Passamaquoddy river. The Malecites were termed Armouchiquois by the French.

The following additional Abnaki tribes are sometimes referred to but they were so small and unimportant comparatively, as to call for no especial notice. They were the Medoctee, the Muanbessik, the Missiassik, and the Accominta. *Vide* "Tribes."

The various tribes of the Abnaki, while possessing many chiefs or sachems, were alike subject to a supreme ruler, known as the Bashaba, up to 1615, when the last representative of this sovereign office was killed in war. The Wewenocks are said to have been the immediate subjects of the Great Bashaba. After his death they settled on the west side of the Sheepscot river, near the lower falls. The residence of the Bashaba was in the vicinity of Pemaquid.

Micmacs. Yet another fierce and warlike tribe, known as the Micmacs, must be mentioned as among the northern Indians. These were the aborigines of Acadia or Nova Scotia, and occupied the great peninsula south of the Bay of Fundy: they were also, according to Schoolcraft, the earliest aborigines of the American Continent to come in contact with Europeans. The French designated them as Souriquois, and they had an intense and unvarying hatred of the Etchemin. The term Micmac means "our allies," or "allies." A definition of the smaller tribes will be found among "The American-Indian Tribes of New England," elsewhere in this volume.

NEW HAMPSHIRE. In New Hampshire there were five principal tribes, viz:—Those on the Piscataqua and its branches, to which the name Newichawannocks belonged, although their main residence was on the Cocheco River, near Dover;—the Pequakets, on Saco River,—the Ossipees, on Lake Ossipee, the Coös Indians, the tribes on the Connecticut River, and the various tribes on the Merrimack, and its tributary streams. Of these the Newichawannocks, the Ossipees, the Pequawkets, and the Coös tribes belonged to the Abnaki nation, and the Pequawkets were the most numerous about the time of the arrival of the Pilgrims in 1620. Little is definitely known of the tribes inhabiting the New Hampshire side of the Connecticut River, but they were probably of a mixed character. The Coös Indians who resided in Grafton and Coös Counties are more or less involved in obscurity, but it it surmised that they constituted a comparatively small tribe, and lived for the most part about the junction of the Upper and Lower Ammonoosuc with the Connecticut River, their main dwelling place being situated at the village of Coös or Coosuc, near the mouth of the Lower Ammonoosuc. They were eventually driven off by the English, in 1704, when they joined the St. Francis Indians.

The Nipmuck tribes of New Hampshire, occupying principally the southern section of the state, constituted with the addition of some of the Massachusetts tribes, what is known as the Pennacook confederacy, of which the illustrious Passaconaway was the Bashaba, or ruling chief. The most powerful of all these tribes lived amid the intervales of Pennacook, where the towns of Bow, Concord, and Boscawen are now situated, in Merrimack County. Of the other Confederated tribes the Nashuas occupied the land, on the Nashua River, and the intervales upon the Merrimack. The Souhegans lived upon the Souhegan River and both banks of the Merrimack above and below the mouth of the Souhegan, the Namaoskeags at the Amoskeag Falls, on the Merrimack, in the vicinity of Manchester, and the Winnepesaukees resided in the neighborhood of the lake of that name. The Massachusetts tribes confederated with these consisted mainly of Agawams (Ipswich), the Wamesits or Pawtuckets, (about Lowell), and the Pentuckets (Haverhill). Passaconaway died in 1660.

In 1850 it was stated that "scarcely an Indian remains in the State."

VERMONT. The territory now represented by the State of Vermont was claimed as hunting-ground by the surrounding tribes, and constituted an area frequently traversed by tribes wandering from north to south, or *vice versa*, as well as intersected by numerous shorter routes in varying directions, and this was, if not the main, at least a contributory factor in preventing the aborigines from making Vermont, to any considerable extent, a permanent residence.

Still there are indubitable proofs that the Indians at an early period, must have resided here, and in considerable numbers The St. Francis tribe on the north — (who had their headquarters at Montreal, Hockhelaga as it was then called)— the Narragansets on the the east,—the Pequots on the south,— the Iroquois or Mohawks on the south-west, (Schenectady, Mohawk River, New York)—were the tribes located in the vinicity of Vermont in comparatively recent times. The territory of the Iroquois, eastward, embraced Lake Champlain and the western part of Vermont, and the Indians on the banks of the Susquehanna, Delaware, Hudson and Connecticut Rivers were in a kind of subjection to them.*

History records the scantiest information concerning the Indians in Vermont, and the Amerind Place and Proper names throughout the Green-Mountain State are so few as to but em-

---

* Dr. S. Williams, *History of Vermont*, 1809.

phasize the fact that the only remaining traces of her aborigines
have almost faded away for ever.

MASSACHUSETTS. Of the *Massachusetts* tribes that bearing
the name of this State had dominion, for the most part, over the
eastern territory adjacent to Massachusetts Bay: there is,
however, little positive evidence forthcoming as to either the
limitations of their territory or their power, as, some time about
1617, the tribe was decimated by a pestilence and thoroughly
disorganized by warfare. Soon after this period their territory
seems to have been divided amongst the Nipmucks, Narragansets
and other tribes. That they formerly sustained a position of importance in the state is evidenced by Gookin who says that their
chief sachem held dominion over many petty governors, as, for
example, those of Weymouth, Neponsit and Punkapoag, and that
his suzerainty extended to Newton Nashaway etc., and as far
as Deerfield, into the heart of the Nipmuck country. Moreover,
Johnson seems to have regarded them more as a confederacy
than as a tribe, and described the group as formerly having
"three kingdoms or sagamoreships, having under them seven
dukedoms or petty sagamores." It also appears that they were
either tributary to, or in alliance with the Narragansets.

According to Hubbard, the mouth of the Charles River was
a rendezvous of all the Indians north and south, and Hutchinson says that the "circle which now makes the harbours of
Boston and Charlestown, round by Malden, Chelsea, Nantasket,
Hingham, Braintree, Weymouth, and Dorchester, was the
Capital of a great sachem;" and the tradition is that he had his
principal seat on a hill * near Dorchester, in the neighborhood
of Squantum. Whether this was the great sachemdom of the
Massachusetts Indians or not cannot now be absolutely stated,
but it may be inferred as very probable. Chickataubit and
Wampatuck, his son, were sachems of this tribe, and the names
of at least eight other sachems are known. The sachemdom of
Chickataubit was at Weymouth. He was probably subject to
the Wampanoags, and his principal residence was at Tehticut,
near Namasket, now Middleborough.

---

* Messatsoosec Hill.

This tribe, it is stated, at one time aggregated 3000 warrior but it is more likely that this number was in excess of all the members of the tribe. Chickataubit died of small-pox about 1633.

Nipmucks. The Nipmuck tribe dwelt, for the most part, in the eastern interior of Massachusetts, and occupied many of the lakes and rivers, especially in Worcester and the adjacent counties. Although the actual limitation of their territory is now indeterminate, it must have been very extensive, as it appears from a XVIIth century map that their boundaries formerly reached as far as Boston, on the east,—as far south as the divisional line of Connecticut and Rhode Island,*— westward as far as Bennington, in Vermont, and in a northern direction at least as far as Concord, New Hampshire, as we have already seen. We are at least assured that they dominated the banks of the Merrimack from Lowell, Mass., to Concord, N. H. One of the favorite seats of the sachems of this tribe was said to have been at Wachusett mountain, near Princeton, in the northern part of Worcester County. Another centre was probably near Medford, Mystic Pond, where their great, and probably last sachem, Nanepashemet, lived, and where he was killed, in 1619.[†]

In addition to the many Indian centres throughout the interior, Nipmuck Sachemdoms also existed at Saugus, (Lynn) at Nahant, Nahumkeag, (Salem), Marblehead, and round the Essex coast. It is, however, probable that many of these originally belonged to the Massachusetts Indians, and that they were transferred to the Nipmucks after the disorganisation of the Massachusetts tribe.

Of the several tribes which inhabited the shores of Massachusetts and Plymouth Bays, the most important was, perhaps, that known as the Wampanoags or Pokanokets who were considered as the third greatest nation in New England when it was settled by the English, and when "the good Massassoit" was their chief sachem or king. It has been asserted that his sovereignty

---

* They also "occupied a territory covering the northern portion of Rhode Island." Sidney S. Rider.

† Shattuck's *History of Concord.*

included all the territory "from Cape Cod and all that part of Massachusetts and of Rhode Island between Narraganset and Massachusetts Bays and inward between Pawtucket and Charles River." Whatever doubt there may be about these limitations, it must be conceded that the Wampanoags exercised some sway over at least, the petty-tribes of the interior, while their own territory extended from Massachusetts Bay to Cape Cod, and through the disputed tracts north of the Narraganset country to the bay bearing the same name.* In this connection it is a curious fact that King Philip, son of Massassoit, and one of his successors, could not induce the Nauset Indians of Cape Cod to take part in his disastrous war of 1675–6.

The principal residence of the great chiefs of the Wampanoags was called Pokanoket, or Mount Hope, now included in Bristol, R. I.

RHODE ISLAND. The *Narraganset* territory was stated † to extend to Pawtucket River, Brookfield, and the Blackstone River, in a northerly direction, westerly to Wickabaug Pond, at West Brookfield, southerly to the ocean and on the east by Narraganset Bay: or as Gookin says‡ about 30 or 40 miles from Sekunk River and Narraganset Bay, including Rhode Island and the other islands in that Bay. Roughly speaking, therefore, their boundaries are represented by the State of Rhode Island as it is to-day.

During the first half of the 17th century the rule of this belligerent and formidable tribe was effectively administered by their two great sachems Canonicus and Miantunnomoh, and, in 1642, they were, perhaps, the strongest, as well as the most warlike of the New England Indians. Although the estimates of their numbers vary very considerably, it is fair to assume that, at this time, the tribe aggregated between 4 and 5000. Their warfare with the Wampanoags, the Pequots, the Mohegans and the English gradually reduced their strength, and the steady advance of the white settlers within the confines of New Eng-

---

* G. L. Austin, *History of Mass.*
† Mass. H. S. Col., 3, 1, 210.
‡ *History of Praying Indians.*

land had so diminished them that, in a little over a century, this great nation was reduced to only a few hundred persons.

The *Nehantics* or *Niantics* constituted a branch of the Narragansetts, and their greatest sachem was Ninigret: the principal residence of the tribe was at Wickabaug, now Westerly, R. I. A section of this tribe resided in Connecticut, when they were known as the Western Niantics.

CONNECTICUT. The Pequots were if not the most numerous, the most formidable as well as the fiercest and bravest of the aborigines of Connecticut. They, together with the Mohegans, belonged originally to the same race as the Mahicans, Mohicanders, or Machanders who resided on the banks of the Hudson. The territory they claimed as their own represented an area of about five hundred square miles, and it extended from the Niantic River, on the west, to Wecapaug, ten miles east of the Pawcatuck River, which divides Connecticut from Rhode Island;— their most northern clans, the Mohegans, extending northward for a distance of about 10 or 12 miles from Long Island Sound: in fine, the suzerainty of their chief sachem was, at one time, said to extend from Narraganset to Hudson River, and all along the Connecticut shore, including Long Island.

Although their numbers have been estimated as aggregating 4000, the probability is that the tribe never exceeded 2000; but almost incessant warfare, and especially the war against the combined Narragansets, Mohegans, and the English, in 1638, completed their overthrow, and they ultimately became the subjects of the white settlers. In 1680, the estimate of the General Court as to the number of the Indians in Connecticut amounted to only 500 warriors as representing about 2500 individuals.

Throughout the State of Connecticut, there were many Indian tribes of comparatively minor importance, such as the Paugussets and Wepawaugs, the Potatucks, the Quinnipiacs, the Hammonassets, and the Tunxis, also the so-called River tribes living on the banks of the Connecticut River, consisting of the Podunks, and the Wangunks: none of these, however, calls for detailed attention here.*

* The respective locations of these tribes will be found in "The Principal American-Indian tribes of New England" elsewhere in this work.

Sassacus was the chief Sachem of the Pequots, and a man who terrorised all the neighboring tribes. He was said to have had 26 sachems under him, and his principal residence was on the River Thames, near New London.

The MOHEGANS. Uncas, Pequot sachem of Mohegan, was a direct descendant of the royal line of the tribe. He married the daughter of Sassacus the Chief Sachem, in 1626, thus strengthening his claims to the tribal sachemdom, and subsequently rebelled against his father-in-law (1634–5?) and was defeated and banished. In 1638 he entered into a treaty with the English in Connecticut, and the Narragansets, and his following, growing in numbers and importance, he was gradually raised to a position of considerable influence and independent power. Uncas died in 1682 or 3. In the history of his race he was probably never excelled in personal bravery, or as a diplomatic strategist.

The territory of the Mohegans, althought its limitations have not been very clearly defined, may be said, roughly, to have extended from a short distance from the Connecticut River, on the south "to a space of disputed country on the north, next the Narragansets." The number of the Mohegans cannot well be estimated with any degree of accuracy. Dr. Williamson in his *History of Maine* computes it as 3000, but as this estimate is made as representing the year 1615, and therefore long before the division of the Pequots took place, it cannot be accepted as either accurate or reliable. My own impression is that the Mohegans were never very numerous—probably under 2000—but that the skilful diplomacy of Uncas enabled them to take a foremost place in the history of the period during which they flourished.

PRAYING INDIANS.

A few words may be devoted to the consideration of the Natick or Praying Indians, a sect developed among the Massachusetts tribe and other converts, in 1646, owing principally to the missionary efforts of Rev. John Eliot, who so far mastered the difficulties of the local Indian dialect as enabled him to translate the Bible into it. From 1646 to 1674 the joint efforts of Messrs. Eliot, Gookin, Mayhew, and others resulted in founding a small school of "Christian Indians" in the following places:—Punkapoag (Stoughton); Hassanamessit (Grafton); Okommakamesit (Marlborough); Wamesit (Tewksbury) Nashobah (Littleton); Magunkaquog (Hopkinton); Manchauge (Oxford); Chabanakongkomun, (Dudley); Maanexit, (Woodstock); Wabquissit (also in Woodstock); Pachachoog (partly in Worcester); Weshakim (Nashaway); Waentug, (Uxbridge); and Natick. In 1674 the missionaries claimed to have converted about 1150 persons, being the aggregate of their converts in all these fourteen towns; but, after 1675 (when Philip's war was in progress), the believers dwindled down to about 300, and, six years after the war, Mr. Eliot could only claim four towns. I am merely stating facts, and make no comment further than to quote the following from Dr Douglass' *Summary* *:— "Mr Eliot," he says, "with immense labor translated and printed our Bible into Indian. It was done with a good, pious design, but it must be reckoned among the *otiosorum hominum negotia:* [the achievements of leisurely men]: it was done in the Natick (Mass.) language. Of the Naticks at present (1745) there are not 20 families subsisting, and scarce any can read. *Cui boni?*"

The foregoing outline of the Amerind tribes of New England will, it is hoped, sufficiently indicate the respective locations of the aboriginal inhabitants. With regard to their aggregate tribal numbers many opinions have been expressed and many estimates given by some of the earlier writers, but most of them have been as rash as extravagant. More careful recent inquiry has elicited the fact that the number of Indians occupying New England, at any time subsequent to the year 1600, has been very much exaggerated, and the writer has been assured by two well-known modern anthropologists, who have made a special study of the matter, that the total number of Indians in New England about the year 1600 did not exceed 24, or 25,000. Their calculations, arrived at independently, are based upon an

---

* Vol. 1, p. 172, *note.*

average of between 75 to 80 souls in each village, and the results are as follows:—

Pequots, ...	2000
Narragansetts, ...	5000
Massachusetts, ...	2500
Wampanoags, ...	3000
Pawtuckets, ...	2000
Mohegans, ...	2000
Maine Indians, ...	2500
All others, ...	2500
Total, .	21,500

The aboriginal inhabitants of the American Continent were foredoomed from the time that European travellers discovered its natural wealth and attractiveness, and began to make settlements upon its productive shores: and when, in 1620, the Pilgrims landed in Plymouth Bay, they brought with them the seeds of a more advanced civilisation which, when cultivated among them, took deep root in the soil, and spread their benignant growths in every direction.

The poor Indians had little chance against such a development, and although, in their primitive and inchoate condition, they were unfitted to withstand the gradually increasing inroads of a more resourceful race, yet the history of their conquests records deeds of bravery,—of self-sacrifice, and of exalted patriotism which no nation has ever excelled.

An opinion, too generally shared, which regards the American-Indian race as mere savages, almost inhuman in their ferocity and cruelty, and without a redeeming feature of any kind, is as untrue as it is unjust. They naturally possessed those characteristics shared by all unenlightened races of men who have been deprived of the elevating influence of civilization, and a high code of ethics, but a careful study of their lives and history shows that, according to their enlightenment, they were actuated by many virtues which, in superior races, count for dignified manhood and nobility of mind. In personal bravery and courage they had few equals, and yet they accepted conquest or punishment with a sublime fortitude and stoicism which scorned to ask for either life or pardon. Equality, freedom and independence constituted the very atmosphere of their being, and in their dealings with their own race the right of each individual and his personal freedom and liberty were universally acknowledged. Judged from our modern standard the principles of morality which governed their lives, if of a lower order, were yet in keeping with their instincts and their environment, and they believed that the crimes of the vicious were punished by the disgrace, contempt, and danger they ensured for transgressors.

In their domestic relationships they were generally faithful and commendable; marital unfaithfulness was regarded as a crime, and Roger Williams gives instances in which married Indians had resided together in mutual trust and quietude for 20, 30, 40, and even 50 years. They treated their children with affection and indulgence, choosing rather to mould their characters by means of reason and persuasion than to use harsher measures.

Robbery, and murder for the sake of robbery, were extremely rare amongst them, and, if they had little idea of the beauty and value of truth, it was because they knew no better. They were loyal to their chiefs and their people, prudent and wise in council, sagacious and intelligent,—extremely hospitable both to strangers and friends, grateful for all benefits received, and ever generous toward each other when fortune seemed to befriend them.

That they were resentful of injury, and revengeful towards their enemies must be admitted, but the conduct of the white settlers towards them was in nowise calculated to repress the activities of Nature's first and dominating law of self-preservation. The history of their gradual extermination forms the darkest pages in the history of their successors, and it was fortunate that the pioneers of New England secured, through the broad-mindedness and generosity of good old Massassoit, the friendliness of the Wampanoags, or another and a different story might have had to be told.

When all that can be said against the Indians has been spoken it must be conceded that they embodied a pure and lofty patriotism for which they fought and died like men and true patriots, and although they had to gradually yield up their possessions and their homes in the land they loved, and to recede and disappear before the advancing wave of civilisation, yet as De Forest says; "We may drop a tear over the grave of the race which has perished, and regret that civilisation and christianity have ever accomplished so little for its amelioration."

ABBREVIATED REFERENCES

H. H. Mass.	Hutchinson's History of Massachusetts Bay.
Mass. Bay Col. Rec.	Massachusetts-Bay Colonial Records.
Mass. H. S. Col.	Massachusetts Historical Society's Collections.
N. H. H. S. Col.	New Hampshire Historical Society's Collections.
R. I. H. S. Col.	Rhode Island Historical Society's Collections.
M. H. S. Col.	Maine Historical Society's Collections.
Conn. H. S. Col.	Connecticut Historical Society's Collections.
Plym. Rec.	Plymouth Colonial Records.
Plym. Rec. Judl.	Plymouth Judicial Records.
Col. Rec.	Colonial Records of Connecticut.
Col. Rec. Lands.	Records of Lands etc., Secretary's Office, Hartford, Conn.
New. Y. Col.	New York Collections.
Hampden Co. Records.	"Indian Deeds." H. A. Wright.
H.-B. of A.-I.	Hand-Book of American Indians: Bureau of Ethnology.
Rider's Map.	Preceding "Lands of Rhode Island," by S. S. Rider.
Smith.	Captain John Smith, Navigator, 1614.
R. W.	Roger Williams.
J. H. T.	Dr. J. Hammond Trumbull.
S. G. D.	Samuel G. Drake.
G.	Moses Greenleaf.
J. G. C.	Hon. J. G. Crawford.
S. G. B.	Stanley G. Boyd. "Indian Local Names."
L. L. H.	Lucius L. Hubbard. "Woods and Lakes of Maine."
Suffolk Rec. or Suff. Rec.	"Suffolk Deeds." Vol. I to XIII.
Church's History.	"Church's Indian Wars, 1675—1704:" edited by S. G. Drake.
De Forest.	"History of the Indians of Conn.," by J. W. DeForest. 1851.
Moh.	Mohegan.
Nip.	Nipmuck.
Narr.	Narraganset.
Quinnip.	Quinnipiac.
Quineb.	Quinebaug.
Peq.	Pequot.

NATIVE AMERICAN
PLACE NAMES
OF
MAINE,
NEW HAMPSHIRE,
& VERMONT

MAINE

Abacotnetic Pond, west branch of Penobscot River (Kettegwe-wick).

Abocadneticook, another form of above. "Stream narrowed by the mountains." L. L. H.

Abagadusset River, Bowdoinham, Sagadahoc Co. : "At the cove, or place of Shelter." J. H. T..

Abagadusset Point, Bowdoinham, Sagadahoc Co.

Abequaduset, another form of foregoing.

Abahos Stream, a branch of Madamiscontis River. "A stream that runs parallel with a big river." L. L. H.

Abbahas Stream, another form of above.

Abatacook Creek.

Abalajackomegus Stream, at foot of K'taadn mountain. "No trees; all smooth." "Bare." L. L. H.

Abalajakomegus Stream.

Abolijakomicus, "Bald Country."

Aboljackarmegas Stream.

Aboljackarmegassic Stream, diminutive of preceding.

Abojedgewak, thoroughfare between North and South Twin-Lakes. "Two currents flow, one on each side of an island, in the thoroughfare." L. L. H.

Aboneisg River, Wiscasset Bay, Sheepscot. *Vide* Aponeg.

Abonnebog, Kennebec River? M. H. S. Col.

Acomes Falls, Androscoggin River. "A place of rest or of stop-ping." S. G. B.

Accominticus, York, York Co.   *Vide* Agamenticus.

Acocisco, the ancient name of Casco Bay.   "A heron" or "crane."
  Vide Aucocisco.   *Kendal's Travels*, 111, 143.

Acquehadongonock Point, Whiskeag.   "Smoked-fish Point."

Acquessuc, Rangeley's.   *Vide* Aquosack, and Acquossuc.   Willis.
Acquossuc.

Agamenticus, York, York Co.   "Small tidal river beyond."
  J. H. T.
Agamenticus Mountain, York Co.   *Vide* Accominticus.
Agamenticus River, York Co.

Aghenibekki River, Sandy River?   *Vide* Meesee Contee and
  Amessaqunticook.   J. H. T.

Agiscohos. *Vide* Aziscoos.   "Little pine trees."   J. G. C.

Agoncy, early aboriginal name for Penobscot Bay.

Aggamoggin Strait, Deerisle.

Agguncia, another name for Norumbega.   John de Laet, *Novus
  Orbis*, pp. 52–55.

Agnascorongan tract.   Kennebec River, M. H. S. Col. 6, 2d, 401.

Aguahadonaneag, aboriginal name of Whiskeag, q. v. M. H. S.
  Col. 4, 2d, p. 245.   *Vide* Aquehadongonock.

Ahmelahcognetercook, both sides of Androscoggin River.   Willis
  The Indian name of Brunswick near the falls.   It is said to
  mean "a place of much game."   Wheeler's *History of Brunswick*, 1878.   *Vide* Amilcungantiquoke.

Ahpmoojeenegamook, same as Baamchenungamo, q. v.   Greenleaf.

Ahsedakwasic, Turner Brook   Upper St. John.   "Place on a
  stream where a stick or rod was pointing to some branch,"
  —as a sign for one to follow in that direction.   L. L. H.

Alamascook River, Bucksport. *Vide* Alamasook. Willis.

Alamasook River, near Orland. *Vide* Alamoosuc. Williamson.

Alamoosuc Pond, near Orland; Hancock Co. "Little dog place."

Alamoosuc River, near Orland.

Alamoosic, Orient, Aroostook Co.

Alamoosic Lake, Orient, Aroostook Co.

Aloostook River. *Vide* Aroostook.

Allagash River, main branch of St. John's.

Allagash Mountains. These words may be contracted from *Allagaskwigamook*, "Bark-Cabin Lake " (near a hunting camp). L. L. H.

Allagundebagog, one of Androscoggin Lakes.

Allahtwkikamoksis Pond, Soubungy Mountain. "Ground where much game has been destroyed."

Alligaskwigamook, Churchill Lake, Allagash River, "Bark-Cabin Lake." L. L. H.

Alligaskwigamoosis, Spider Lake.

Alligaskwigamooksis.

Allaquash River. *Vide* Allagash.

Alna? early name of Dresden, Lincoln Co.

Amaeconti, near Androscoggin.

Amaseconti River. *Vide* Amesookkatti.

Amasquanteg. *Vide* Amesookkatti and Amessagunticook.

Ambajeejus. *Vide* Ambejijis.

Ambajeejus Falls.

Ambajemackomas, Elbow Lake, near North Twin Lake. "Little Cross Pond." L. L. H.

Ambejijis, one of the Penobscot Lakes, so called probably from two large, round rocks in the lake, one on top of the other. L. L. H.

Ameriscoggin, derived from words signifying "a fishing place on the river." J. H. T.   Same as Androscoggin, q. v.

Amesookkatti, an Abnaki village, near the river Aghenibekki. Rasle.

Amessagunticook. *Vide* Amessookkatti.

Amigoupontook. *Vide* Amitygouponticook.

Amilcungantiquoke, St. Francis, Aroostook.   "Banks of the river abounding in dry meat." (Venison.)

Amisceskeag Point, Kittery, York.

Amitigouponticook, Lewiston Falls.

Amityouponook. Willis.

Ammarescoggen, same as Androscoggin, q. v.

Ammeguntick Lake.   M. H. S. Col. 1st series.

Ammon-Congin, Indian Planting-ground at Cumberland Mills. "Fish-drying." *Indian Bulletin*, 1867.

Ammongungon River, Falmouth, Casco Bay.

Amobscot. *Vide* Muscongus : probably a corruption of Remobscus, q. v. "York Records," XIII, p. 836.

Amoscoggin, same as Androscoggin, q. v.   "A Fishing-place."

Amoscommun, same as Androscoggin, q. v.   "Fishing-place for alewives :" "Fish-spearing place."

Anboljokomagassick. *Vide* Aboljackarmegassic.   "Bald country." G.

Androscoggin, said to be a corruption of Anasagunticook. Probably derived from words signifying a "fishing-place on the river." J. H. T.

Androscoggin River, a branch of the Kennebec.

Aneksassisscuk Island, Penobscot River; "Ant Island." G.

Anghemaktikoos, early name for Agamenticus.

Anmecangin Falls, Lisbon Falls.   "Much fish."

Annabessacook Pond, Monmouth, Kennebec Co.

Annabescook Pond. Willis.

Annabasook Pond. Willis.

Apananawapeske River, "12 miles from Pamassoc," q. v. near
Meecombe, Pemaquid.

Apistama, the sea-board from Casco Bay eastward.

Apmogeregamook Lake, Allagash River. *Vide* Appmoojeenequamook. Willis.

Aponeg River, Sheepscot River.

Apmoojenegamook, Chamberlain Lake, Allagash River; "Cross
lake." L. L. H.

Appmoojeenequamook. *Vide* Baamcheenungamook.

Appowick River, "in the Bashaba's dominions," near Pemaquid.
Purchas' Pilgrimage, 1628.

Aquadocta, Indian village, west of Saco and Casco, 1690.

Aquahadonaneag, same as Whiskeag, q. v.

Aquehadongonock. *Vide* Acquehadongonock.

Aquaquamset River, east of Kennebec. Suffolk Rec., 494,
vol. IV, 1661.

Aquosack. *Vide* Acquessuc and Acquossuc.

Arambec, a synonym for Norumbega or Norumbegua, a place
supposed to have existed at an early period at or near Pemaquid. The meaning of the word is said to be "chief city or
capital." Sewall's, "Ancient Dominion of Maine."

Aransoak, Kennebec River from lake to Norridgewock. *Vide*
Orantsoak.

Aresiket River, Casco Bay.

Arroseag. *Vide* Arrowsic. Sullivan, 145.

Arrozeek. *Vide* Arrowsic.

Arroseg. *Vide* Arrowsic. *Vide* Rowsick.

Arrosic. *Vide* Arrowsic. Sullivan, 145.

Arrowsick. *Vide* Arrowsic.

Arrowsic Island, Sagadahoc.

Aroostook Co.

Aroostook River, Aroostook Co. *Vide* Aloostook and Oolastook.
"Beautiful River."

Arrockaumecook, on Androscoggin River. "A place of dried
meat." (Venison). Willis.

Arumsunkhungan Island, Penobscot River. "Where they catch
alewives."

Arumsunkumgan village.

Asabumbeduco River, Kittery, York.

Ashamahaga River, Pemaquid. *Purchas' Pilgrimage,* 1628.
(Hakluyt's Papers).

Asnela, a little island in Penobscot River. Name derived from
that of Sachem,—Assen or Ossen.

Assabenbeduck, Quamphegan Falls, South Berwick.

Assabumbedoc.

Asticou, near North-east Harbor, Mount-Desert Island. Name
probably derived from that of Sachem.

Aswaguscawadic, a branch of the Mattawamkeag. "A place
where, on account of the distance, one drags his canoe through
a stream, rather than carry it." L. L. H.

Atean Pond, Moose River. Named after an Indian family, and
formerly, after a chief. L. L. H.

Attean Pond.

Attebemeuck Island, Cherry Island, Penosbcot River.

Aucocisco. *Vide* Acocisco, "a heron or crane."

Aumaughcawgen, on Kennebec River : ancient name of Androscoggin.

Aumoughcawgin, "Fishing-place Weir," or "Beaver Dam." Capt. John Smith, 1616.

Awanganis, Priestley Lake, Allagash River. "Lake or water reached from a river by cutting across country up a brook, and thence by land, instead of going around and up the outlet of the lake." L. L. H.

Awasoos Island, Penobscot River. "Bear Island." G.

Aziscoos Mountain, Oxford Co. *Vide* Agiscohos.

Aziscoos Falls, Oxford Co.

Aziscoos River. Oxford Co.

B

Baamchenungamis.

Baamcheenungamook, Chamberlain Lake, Allagash River.

Baamchenungamo, "Lake that is crossed," G. "Cross Lake," "Crosswise." L. L. H.

Baamchenunquamook.

Bagaduce. *Vide* Bigaduce and Major-Bigwaduce.

Bagadoose.

Bakungunahik Island, "Crooked Island." G.

Bamedumpkok Lake, "Sandy-barred Pond." G.

Bamonewengamok, Cross Lake, head of Allagash. *Vide* Baamchenungamis. Willis.

Bascahegan Lake, Topsfield, Washington Co.

Bascohegan Lake, Topsfield, Washington Co.

Bascanhegan Lake, Topsfield, Washington Co.

Baskahegan Stream, a branch of the Mattawamkeag. "A branch stream that turns right down." L. L. H.

Bauneg Beg, Berwick boundary, Sanford. *Vide* Bonabisse.

Bedabedec, early name of Owl's-head, Penobscot Bay. Willis.

Beegwatook, Pushaw Pond, near Bangor. "Big-bay place." L. L. H.

Beemsquamkeetook Lake, Penobscot River. "Quick, smooth water." G.

Bigaduce, the name of Castine and neighborhood about 1689.

Biguaduce Peninsula. *Vide* Marche Bagyduce.

Bigwaduce Peninsula.

Big Tunk mountain, Cherryfield, Washington Co.

Bokajenesquis Island. Jug Island. G.

Bombazee Rips, on the Kennebec River.

Bonabisse Pond, Berwick boundary, Sanford.

Bonnebeag Pond, Berwick boundary, Sanford. *Vide* Bauneg Beg. Willis.

Bosquenoosick Island, Burying ground for Mohawks. G.

Bosquenuguk Island, Broken Island. Penobscot River. G.

Brassua, a lake on Moose River. Suggested to mean "Frank," from an Indian chief.

Brassaway.

Bunganuck. "Maine Register."

Bunganuc, Cumberland, Cumberland Co.

Bunganut Pond, Lyman, York Co.

Bunganut Pond, Alfred, near Sanford, York Co. M. H. S. Col. Vol. 3.

Bungernuck Pond, Alfred, York Co.

Bungernuck Pond, Hartford, Oxford Co.

Bungernuck Stream, Hartford, Oxford.

These names illustrate some of the difficulties of localization, owing to different records of different authors.

Bunganock, History of Brunswick, Topsham and Harpswell, p. 553.

Bungonengamock River, South side of Brunswick. Willis.

Burganunganock River, "flowing into Maquoit Bay :" "Highbank Brook."

Bungomungomug River, "flowing into Maquoit Bay."

Busseck, Sagadahoc. M. H. S. Col. 6, 2d, 401.

C

Cabbadetus, Round Pond Village, Bristol. Lincoln Co. Records.

Canasixet River, Mill River, Sheepscot. *Vide* Cavesisix.

Canesixet Falls, Scarborough.

Cancumgomock, one of summits of Russell mountains, Somerset Co.

Cancumgomock Lake, Chesuncook, west branch of Penobscot. *Caucomgomoc* Lake, Chesuncook, "Big-gull lake." L. L. H.

Capaneldagan. Willis.

Capeangusset, Cape Anagusset, Swan Island.

Capecorpus, early name of Mousam River. Mass. H. S. Col. Vol. III, p. 6 (1610.)

Capenawaghen, same as Cape Newaggen.

Capesseck Falls, Falmouth, York Co. "York Records," XIII, p. 362.

Capipissoke Falls, Falmouth, York Co. "York Records."

Capisick Falls, Falmouth, York Co. "York Records."

Capissick Falls, Falmouth, York Co. "York Records."

Capissick River, southeast of mouth of Stroudwater. *Vide* Kepisicke, Little River. Williamson, 1, p. 264, note.

Capmanwagan, now Southport.

Caratunk, on Kennebec River.

Caratunk Lake, Caratunk, Kennebec River.

Carratunk, Concord. "Maine Register."

Caribou, Aroostook Co.

Caribou River, Aroostook Co.

Caribou Bog, Crystal, Aroostook Co.

Carrabasset River, Eustis, Franklin Co.

Carrabasset Falls, Anson, Somerset Co.

Carrabasset Rapids, Anson, Somerset Co.

Carrartoank Falls, Kennebec. *Vide* Caratunk. Willis.

Carrituck Plantation, Somerset Co. "Place where the water forms a semi-circle round the land."

Casco, early name of Portland. "Goes round, like a collar." J. G. C. Said also to be derived from Aucocisco, meaning "a resting place," or "a crane."

Casco Bay, Cumberland Co.

Casco River, Cumberland Co.

Catawamteak, Rockland, Knox Co. "Great landing-place."

Cathance River, Bowdoinham, Sagadahoc Co.

Cathance Point, Bowdoinham. *Vide* Kathahnis.

Cathaneu River, "Bent" or "Crooked."

Cathanisk, Denny's River, Washington Co. P. E. Vose.

Cauccow Cove, Rasthegon Island, Sagadahoc.

Caucongamock Lake. *Vide* Cancumgonock. Willis.

Cavesisix River, between Damariscotta and Sheepscot Rivers.

Chamcook Hills, north of Passamaquoddy Bay. N. B.

Chamcook Lake, north of Passamaquoddy Bay, N. B.

Chamqussabamtook Lake, tributary to Allagash. *Vide* Chemquasabamticook.

Cheaplawgan Lake. Willis.

Chebeague Island, Harpswell, Cumberland Co. "Great waters" or "great expanse of water." *Vide* Ch'ebeag and Shebeag.

Chebeag.

Chebeguadose, a village on the Penobscot. *Purchas' Pilgrimage,* 1628.

Chebiscodego Island, Casco Bay: former name of Great Chebeague.

Chebogardinac? "a high hill."

Cheburn, West Quoddy head.

Cheemanahn. "Great Island." G.

Chegoney Island, Sagadahoc. Same as Sagosett, q. v.

Chekachenegabit, west branch of Penobscot. G.

Chemquasabamticook Lake, tributary to the Allagash. L. L. H.

Chemquasabanticook Stream, "stream of a large lake."

Chenosbec, name for Chesuncook, q. v. It may mean "great outlet place."

Chenbesic.

Cheputneticook Lakes, Vanceborough, Washington Co. "Great hill lake."

Cheputnaticook Stream, Schoodic.

Cheputnatecook.

Chesuncook Lake, west branch of Penobscot. "The biggest lake" — on the Penobscot. It may mean "Great discharge place." L. L. H.

Chetookook. *Vide* Chesuncook. G.

Chevacovett, ancient name of Pemaquid and Sheepscot.

Chevacovett River (Nichols River) branch of Sheepscot.

Chiboctous River, Penobscot. Biard.

Chicopee, York Co.

Chickawaukie, Tolman's Pond, Rockland, Knox Co.; "sweet water."

Chickawakie, Tolman's Pond, Rockland, Knox Co.

Chickawauka, Tolman's Pond, Rockland, Knox Co.

Chicumskook, Grindstone Falls, Penobscot, "Big Falls" or "Big-boulder place." L. L. H.

Chignecto Bay, Bay of Fundy.

Chignecto Cape, Bay of Fundy.

Chimkazaooktook, branch of St. John. "Big black stream." L. L. H.

Chimquassabumtook. *Vide* Chemquasabamticook.

Chimmenticook River, Aroostook Co.

Chinskheegan, Ktaadnquoh, Mount Ontop.

Chiputneticook. *Vide* Cheputneticook.

Chusquisack River, near Wecustogo. "York Records."

Cinebaque, same as Kennebec. M. H. S. Col. 7, 2d, 431.

Cobeskoute Lake, Kennebec Co.; "sturgeon-spearing place." *Vide* Cobbossecontee.

Cobbasseeconteag Lake, Kennebec Co. "Land where sturgeons are taken." Willis.

Cobbossecontee Lake, Kennebec Co. "Where there was plenty of sturgeons. J. H. T. "Place where sturgeons are taken." Mass. H. S. Col. Vol. 3, p. 6.

Cobbosse, Gardiner. "Maine Register."

Cobscook Falls, Pembroke, Washington Co. "Falls, or rough water." L. H. H.

Cobscook Bay. Pembroke, Washington Co.

Cobscook Stream, Pembroke, Washington Co. "Sturgeon-catching place." J. H. T.

hnewaga Pond, Monmouth, Kennebec Co.
Cocknewegan Pond, Monmouth, Kennebec Co.

Collegewidgwock, Blue-hill, near Union River.

Comphegan, same as Quamphegan, q. v. "York Records," 1, 36.

Condeskeag, Bangor.
Conduskeag, Bangor.

Copones Island, Casco Bay.
Copsecook. *Vide* Cobscook.

Cowseagan Narrows, on Sheepscot River. M. H. S. Col. Vol. 2, pp. 235-6.
Cowsegan River, runs into Sheepscot.

Crokemago, small province at head of Saco River. It contained one town, probably Pegwaket. Williamson, Vol. 1, p. 10, note.

Crummet? Somerville, Lincoln Co.

Culcusso Mountain, Somerset Co.

Cumbolasse Ponds, Lincoln, Penobscot Co.

Cupsuptic Lake, Oxford Co.

Cupsuptic River, Oxford Co. The act of "drawing a seine while fishing."

Curvo Stream? Salem, Franklin Co.

Cushenoc, Augusta, same as Cushnoc. "The running-down place."
Cushnoc, Augusta.

Custogo, West Yarmouth. Willis.

Cussabexis Pond, near Chesuncook Lake. "The little swift water." L. L. H.

Cussenocke. *Vide* Cushnoc.

D

Damariscotta, Bristol, Lincoln Co. "Alewife Place."

Damariscotta River, Bristol, Lincoln Co. "River of little fishes," or "The river where the fishes flock or rush." "Fish-place." Willis.

Damariscotta Islands, mouth of Damariscotta River. Possibly the "Tamiscot" of Heylin, 1645. Willis.

Donaqua, the former name of land lying between Penobscot and Union Rivers.

E

Ebauhuit Island, Campobello, N. B.

Ebeeme Mountains, Moosehead Lake, "where they get high-bush cranberries." L. L. H.

Ebeemin, same as Ebeeme.

Ebenecook Village, Lincoln Co. "Bread place," or "high cranberry place."

Ebenecooke Harbour, at Cape Newagen Island. *Vide* Menicuk.

Ebhops River, Woodville, Penobscot Co.

Edgemaroggan Reach, near Sedgwick, Brookville.

Eggemoggin Reach, Penobscot Bay.

Egamagen Reach. M. H. S. Col. Vol. 1, 3d, 448.

Ehusquisack River, Wescustogo, North Yarmouth. *Vide* Chusquisack. "York Records" XII, part 1, p. 112.

Elandamookganopskitschwak Falls, east branch of Penobscot. "Stair Falls." L. L. H.

Epituse, probable name of mainland on which Boothbay stands. Mentioned in deed of Damariscove, 1685.

Eptchedgewak, thoroughfare between North and South Twin-lakes, Penobscot. "Where two currents, coming from different directions, meet." L. L. H.

Erascohegan, Great Island, Harpswell, Cumberland Co.

Escutassis Pond, Burlington, Penobscot Co.

Escutassis Pond, Little, Lowell, Penobscot Co. "Small trout." L. L. H.

Eskulassis Pond, Lowell, Penobscot Co.

Escutassis Stream, Lowell, Penobscot Co. "Small trout."

Eskweskwewadjo, Bald Mountain, Katahdin Range. "She-bear mountain." L. L. H.

Etasiiti, ancient name of Wilson Pond, Moosehead Lake. "Where they had a great fight," or "destruction ground." L. L. H.

G

Gambo, Gorham, Cumberland. Pierce's "Gorham," p. 41.

Gebeag Islands, Casco Bay. (anciently Chebeague.)

Genesagarumsis Lake, easternmost of Schoodic Lakes.

Georgeekeag, Thomaston.

Godmorrocke, marshland, northeast of Piscataqua, Kittery. "York Records," vol. 3, p. 97, 98.

Guonitogon, "Long River," early Abnaki name of Connecticut River.

Great Jebege Island, "near Merecanneeg." *Vide* Chebeaque.

Gumscook Pond. Willis.

Gunasquamekook, an Abnaki village (Passamaquoddy) H-B. of A-I. Vol. 1, p. 4.

Gyobscot Point, Sagadahoc Co.

H

Hackmatack Lake, or Little Seavey, Wesley, Washington Co.

Hanesicket Bay, Freeport, Cumberland Co.

Harraseeket, Freeport, Cumberland Co.

Harraseeket River, Freeport, Cumberland Co.

Harrickissecke, Freeport, Cumberland Co. "York Records," 3,130.

Heggomeito, near Passage Point, York. "York Records," XII, Part 2, p. 323.

Hemanockwanargum, Pembroke Lake.   P. E. Vose of Dennysville.

Hoagomore Cove, Greenland.

Hockomock Point, near old harbor, Swan's Island. *Vide* Namokanok.

Hockomock Head, Woolwich, Sagadahoc Co.

Hockamock Island, Oldtown, above Penobscot. "High land,—kind of a lump."

Hockamock Bay. Sheepscot? M. H. S. Col. 2, 2d, 247.

Hockomocking Point or Neck, Muscongus.

Hogamockcook Point, Greenland. "York Records."

Hoosac Mount, at Cornish, York Co.

I

Imnarkuan, an Abnaki village, Passamaquoddy, H-B. of A-I. 1, p. 4.

J

Jameco Path, Scarborough.

Jataska Lake, Oxford Co.

Jebaskadiggin, one of the Casco-Bay Islands. *Vide* Sebascodegan.

Jebege, Great Island, Harpswell, Cumberland. *Vide* Chebeague.

Jeremisquam Island, Westport, near Wiscasset, Lincoln Co. "The Island of Jeremy, who lives by the water,"—meaning "the island of water-creeks." Sewall.

Jewonke Neck, near Westport, Lincoln Co.

Jewanke Neck, near Westport, Lincoln Co. Probate Records.

K

Kabaumkeag, Lubec, Eastport. P. E. Vose.

Kadesquit, early name of Bangor. M. H. S. Col. 4, 2d, 90.

Kahgognamock, or Black River,—source of west tributary of Penobscot.

Kahkoguamock Lake, same as Caucomgomock, q. v. "Big-gull lake."

Kahnonahjik, Long Island, Penobscot River. G.

Karsaootuk Stream, North Maine; "Black River," or "Pine Stream."

Kassanunganumkeag, Elaware Rips. G.

Katachinoe, one of forks of Penobscot River.

Katahdin Mountain, Piscataquis Co. "The biggest mountain." *Vide* K'taadn.

Katapskenegan Lake, west branch of Penobscot.

Katapskonegan Falls, west branch of Penobscot, "a carry over a ledge" or "big ledge carry." L. L. H.

Katawamkisway River, same as Memkeeswee, q. v.

Kathahnis River. Bowdoinham. *Vide* Cathance; "crooked."

Kawapskitchwak, Machias west River. "Sharp rough rips" or "rocky stream." L. L. H.

Kebo Mountain, Hancock Co.

Kedumcook, Vaughan Brook, Hallowell.

Kenderquit, former name of Bangor, Penobscot.

Kenduskeag, former name of Bangor, Penobscot. "The place of eels." Willis.

Kenduskeag River, Penobscot : "Little eel River," or "place for taking salmon."

Kennebago River, near Rangeley, Franklin Co.
Kennebago Falls, near Rangeley, Franklin Co.
Kennebago Lake, near Rangeley, Franklin Co.
Kennebago Mountains, near Rangeley, Franklin Co.

Kennebec village (Norridgewock), named for great chief, Kennebis, or means "long-water place," or "long river."
Kennebec River.

Kennebunk Pond, York.

Kennebunk, York.

Kennebunk Beach, York.

Kennebunkport, York.

Kepisicke River. *Vide* Capisick and Capissick. "York Records," XII, part 2, p. 311.

Kerdoormeorp, at Pittston, Kennebec Co.

Ketangheanyche, Abnaki village, near mouth of Kennebec River. M. H. S. Col. V, p. 156.

Kettegwewick, west branch of Penobscot. "Great stream place." L. L. H.

Kezar River, Fryeburg, Oxford Co. Named from an old hunter, who lived in the vicinity.

Kezar Pond.

Kineo Mountain, Moosehead Lake, Piscataquis Co.

Kineo, Moosehead Lake, Piscataquis Co.

Klaganissecook village, Mattawamkeag River.

Klaganissecook Falls, Mattawamkeag River. "Narrow, like a door." L. L. H.

Kobossee Island. "Sturgeon Island." G.

Kokadjeweemgwasebem, Roach Pond, Moosehead Lake. "Kettle-mountain Lake."

Kokadjeweemgwasebemsis, Spencer Pond, Moosehead Lake. "Kettle-mountain Pond." L. L. H.

Kokadjo, western peak of Spencer mountains; "Kettle-mountain." L. L. H.

Kollegewidgewock, Indian name for Blue-hill Bay. Willis.

Kousaki Lake, said to be source of St. Croix River. M. H. S. Col. 6, 2d, 237.

K'taadn mountain, Piscataquis Co. The "biggest mountain."

K'taadnquoh, Ontop mountain, "of or belonging to Katahdin range."

Kukunsook Lake, Pushau Lake. G.

Kurremuck, spruce creek, Kittery.

Kussuskook Lake, Hemlock Lake. G.
Kussuskook Stream, Hemlock stream. G.
Kussuskook Island, Hemlock Island. G.

Kwanatacogomahso, Poland Pond—tributary to Caucomgomoc Lake. L. L. H.

Kwanoksagamaik, Loon Lake, Caucomgomuc. "Peaked or pointed lake." L. L. H.

Kwanosagamaik, Webster Lake, on Penobscot, east branch. L. L. H.

Kweueuktonoonkhegan, Moose River. "Snow-shoe River." L. L. H.

Kynybequy, ancient name of Kennebec (Quinnebequi) charter of King Charles 1, 1639.

L

Lacassecomecook. *Vide* Allagaskwigamook (1795). "Bark-cabin place."

Lapomique, a branch of Aroostook. "Rope stream" (crooked).
Lapompeag.

Lechock River, "5 leagues east of Penobscot." H. H. Mass. III, p. 13.

Lett Island? Old town, Penobscot. Levingston, 1710.

Loon Pond, Litchfield, Kennebec Co. *Vide* Kwanoksagamaik.

Loshtock, or Long River, Indian name of St. John's River. "Wide and shallow." Hanson's *"History of Gardiner."*

Lunksoos Mountain, Penobscot, "Indian devil," or "Catamount."

Lunksoos Stream, east branch of Penobscot.

M

Machagoney Point, Falmouth. "York Records," XII, part 1, p. 113.

Machigonne, Portland or Casco Neck. "Bad clay," or "Knee"or "elbow" (from curve of peninsula).

Magegunuck Neck, Falmouth. "York Records," XII, part 1, p. 113.

Machias, Washington Co.

Machias River, Washington Co. "Bad small falls," or "Bad little place."

Machias Bay, Washington Co.

Machiasport, Washington Co.

Macheeweesis Falls, "Bad Falls." G.

Machwahoc, Aroostook Co. "Beaver place?"

Machwahoc Stream, Aroostook Co. "Bog-brook." L. L. H.

Macwahoc, Aroostook Co.

Macwahoc Stream, Aroostook Co.

Macwakook, Aroostook Co.

Madagamus Hill, near Belfast, Waldo Co. "The trace of the snow-shoes."

Madagascal, Burlington, Penobscot.

Madagascal Pond, Burlington, Penobscot.

Maddambettox Mountain, Rockland, Knox Co.

Maddunkeunk River, Chester, Penobscot. "It goes up rapid from the mouth of the brook."

Medunkeeunk. *Vide* Namadunkeeunk.

Medunkeeunk Falls, Chester.

Madamiscontis Stream, Penobscot. *Vide* Mattamiscontis.

Madamiscondus Stream, "where there has been plenty of alewives."

Madamiskontis Lake.

Madamiscomtis Stream.

Madanamkook Island, Sandy Island, Penobscot.

Madanankook River.

Matanaucook, Lower Penobscot; "Place of bad islands."   L. L.H. *Vide* Metanawcook, Metanawkeag, etc.

Madawamkeag Lake, Oxford Co. *Vide* Mattawamkeag.

Madawaska, Aroostook Co.

Madawaska River, east of St. John, near Little Falls. "Porcupine place," or "where one river enters another."   L. L. H.

Madibpar Falls, "Flint-stone Falls."   G.

Madnaguk Island, Lincoln Island, Penobscot.

Madoamuk.

Madoamok Point, east of Masconks, "York Records," 8, 177.

Maductic Falls, St. John's River.

Medunctic Point, St. John's River.

Madusnekeag, tributary of St. John's. *Vide* Medusnekeag and Meduxnekeag.   Willis.

Magawok Bay, near Maquoit.   Willis.

Magegunuck Neck, Falmouth. *Vide* Machagoney.

Magesemanussick Falls, York Co. "York Records," VIII, p. 177.

Magocook Bay, near Maquoit. *Vide* Magawok.

Magguadaric River, Washington Co.

Magorgoomagoosuck, "7 mile Brook," Vassalborough.

Maguncook. *Vide* Mousam River.

Magurrewock Lake, West, Calais, Washington Co.

Magurrewock Lake, East, Calais, Washington Co.

Mahklicomgonoc, Pleasant Lake, Allagash : "Hard-wood land lake." L. L. H.

Mahkonlahgok, "The Gulf," near K'taadn. "A hole in the river." L. L. H.

Mahnagwanegwasebem, Rainbow Lake, Penobscot, Translation of English name : not genuine Indian.

Mahnekebahntic, Caribou Lake, Chesuncook. "Where they got cedar-bark for packs." L. L. H.

Majaobskoos, Pomoohah's (Devil's) rock.

Major-Bigwaduce, Plantation name of Penobscot (Castine). *Vide* Marche Bagyduce, and Biguaduce. "At the bad shelter-place." Rasle and J. H. T.

Majuumquassabam Pond, "Bad Pond." G.

Makwamkusk, Red Beach, Eastport.

Malagoe Island, Isles of Shoals.

Malaquash, Lunenburg, N. S.

Merliquash, Lunenburg, N. S.

Mamasunquobscook River, "Rough Stone Stream." G.

Manahneekook, "River full of Islands." G.

Manan Islands, "An Island."

Manahnook, "Grand Manan." P. E. Vose.

Manaskoos, Green Island, Penobscot.   G.

Mandawesso Island, Hedgehog Island.   G.

Manheigin Island, mouth of Penobscot.   Des Barre's Map.   *Vide* Monahigan.

Manickoe Point, Newton, Casco.

Maquait Bay, Brunswick, Cumberland Co.

Maquoit, Brunswick, Cumberland Co.

Maquarook River, St. John's, "Birch stream."   G.

Maranacook Lake, Readfield, Kennebec.

Maranocook Lake, Readfield, Kennebec.

Marche Bagyduce.   *Vide* Major Bigwaduce, and Biguaduce.

Marchissis Mount, Chase Mount.

Mardarmeskunteag, Damariscotta, "Young shad pool."

Margalloway, English in Indian guise.

Maroonscook Pond, Cobbessecontee.   Willis.

Masardis River, Aroostook Co.

Mascamp, near Alfred, York Co.

Masconks, "York Records," VIII, p. 177.

Masherosqueck, an Abnaki village, in 1616.   Smith, pp. 13, 14, 213, 214.

Masquaseecook Lake, Penobscot River, "Birch Stream."   G.

Massabeseck, Waterborough.   *Vide* Massabeisic.

Massabeisic, Alfred or Sanford, York Co.

Massakiga, Abnaki village.   *Purchas' Pilgrimage,* 1628.

Mastomquoog Island, St. George's River.

Matagamook, Grand Lake, E. Penobscot.   "The old exhausted lake."   L. L. H.

Matagamooksis, Second Lake, E. Penobscot. Diminutive of preceding.

Matagmnon Lake, Penobscot River, Aroostook. *Vide* Mattagamon.

Matanaucook, Penobscot River. "Place of bad lands." *Vide* Matanacook.

Matakeunk Pond, Lee, Penobscot Co. *Vide* Mattakeunk. Willis.

Matakeunk Stream, Lee, Penobscot Co. *Vide* Mattakeunk. Willis.

Mathebestuck Hills, Camden, Knox Co. *Vide* Mattubesic and Medambattec.

Matinicus Isle, "10 miles east of Matinic," Knox Co.

Matinicus Rock, "10 miles east of Metinic Island," Knox Co.

Mattabesec. *Vide* Mattubesic : refer also to Conn. and N. H.

Mattagamon Lake, Penobscot River. *Vide* Montagamon.

Mattagoodus, a tributary of Penobscot; "bad landing for canoes" or "meadow-ground." L. L. H.

Mattagordus River, at Prentiss, Penobscot Co.

Mattakeunk Pond, Lee, Penobscot Co. *Vide* Matakeunk.

Mattakeunk Stream, Lee, Penobscot Co. *Vide* Matakeunk.

Mattamiscontis River, tributary of Penobscot; "where there has been plenty of alewives." J. H. T. *Vide* Madamiscomtis, etc.

Mattanacook Ponds, Lincoln, Penobscot. "Place of bad islands."

Mattanacook stream.

Mattanawcook, M. H. S. Col. VII, p. 103. *Vide* Matanaucook, Metanawcook, etc.

Mattawamkeag River, Oxford Co. *Vide* Metawamkeag and Madawamkeag.

Mattawamkeag Lake, "Down where a stream empties into the main river." "Gravelly bed," or "place beyond the gravel or sand bar." L. L. H.

Mattubesic Mountain, Rockland, Knox Co. *Vide* Maddambettox.

Maun Hill, Mexico, Oxford Co.

Mavosheen, earliest name of Maine, 1602?

Mavoosheen, earliest name of Maine.

Meaumkeag, near Kitt's Island, Kennebec.

Mecadacut, old name of Owl's Head. *Vide* Medambattic. Smith, 1616.

Mechisses, old name for Machias, q. v. Mass. H. S. Col. Vol. III (1810).

Mechisses River, Mass. H. S. Col. Vol. III (1810).

Medambattic Hill or Mountain, near Camden. *Vide* Mathebestuck, and Mecadacut.

Meddybemps, Washington Co.

Meddybemps River, Washington Co.

Meddybemps Falls, Washington Co.

Meddybempsook, Washington Co. P. E. Vose.

Medoctec, Abnaki village (Maliseet).

Medomac River, Appleton, Knox Co.

Medunkaunk, Chester, Penobscot Co. *Vide* Namadunkeehunk.

Medunkeeunk River, Chester, Penobscot Co.

Medunkeeunk Falls, Chester, Penobscot Co.

Meduncook, Friendship town, Knox Co.

Medusnekeag River, a tributary of the lower St. John.

Meduxnekeag River, near Woodstock, "where the people go out" (from the woods.) L. L. H.

Meduxnekeag Lake, Linneus, Aroostook Co.

Meecombe, Abnaki village on the Apananawpeske River. q. v. H-B. of A-I. Vol. 1, p. 5.

Meeseecontee, Farmington Falls, Sandy River, "where there is plenty of alewives or herrings."

Meesokdowhok Lake, "Burnt land?" G.

Meesokdowhok Stream.

Meesucontee. *Vide* Amesookkatti.

Megkwagagamik, Mud Pond, Allagash. "Marsh Pond." L. L. H.

Megkwakangamocsis, Harrow Pond. "Marsh Pond." L. L. H.

Megkwahlagas, near Lower Penobscot. "Red Hole" or "Red Rock." L. L. H.

Megquier Hill, Poland Springs, Androscoggin Co.

Megunticook, Camden, Knox Co.

Megunticook Mountain, Camden, Knox Co.

Megunticook River, Camden, Knox Co.

Megunticook Lake, Camden, Knox Co.

Melapswagamoc, Joe Merry Lake, Penobscot. "Large rock lake." L. L. H.

Meloxswangarmo, corruption of above.

Memkeeswee Stream, eastern bound of Maine. *Vide* Katwamkisway.

Mempticook Stream, eastern bound of Maine.

Menannah Bay, between Monhegan and Manannah Island.

Menannah Island, south of Monhegan.

Menhaneekek, Ragged Lake, near Chesuncook. "Place of many islands."

Meniceneag, Harpswell, North Yarmouth. *Vide* Merryconeag.

Menikoe Point, beyond Portland Neck. M. H. S. Col. Vol. 1, p. 77.

Menicuk, early form of Ebenecook, q. v.

Mericaneeg, now Harpswell, N. Yarmouth, same as Merryconeag, q. v.

Merrinege Neck, Casco Bay.

Merryconeag, Harpswell Neck, Cumberland Co.

Mesakketesagewick, Socatean Stream, meaning "half-burnt land and half-burnt timber with the stream separating them."

Mesiginagoske, Indian Island, Passamaquoddy.

Meskaskeeseehunk, north branch Mattawamkeag. "Little spruce brook." L. L. H.

Meskeekwagamasic, Black Pond, Caucomgonoc. "Grassy Pond." L. L. H.

Messalouskee River. M. H. S. Coll. 4, 2d, 366.

Messalonski Pond, Sidney, Kennebec Co.

Messeelonskee, Emerson Stream, Waterville.

Messotoocus, Smith Brook, Mattawamkeag.

Metanawcook River, Penobscot River. "Place of bad lands."

Metanawkeag River (Indian form). *Vide* Matanaucook, etc.

Metanegwis, St: Croix Island. M. H. S. Col. Vol. 2, 3d, 109.

Metawamkeag River, Penobscot River. *Vide* Mattawamkeag.

Metawarmet, Boothbay.

Metgarmette.   Willis.

Mgwasebemsistook, Russell Stream, north of Moosehead Lake. "Stream of a little lake." L. L. H.

Millinokett Lake, Penobscot Co. "Having no shape;" "having many coves," or "Place full of islands."

Millininoketsis, one of the Aroostook Lakes. Diminutive of preceding.

Minnehonk Lake.

Mispecky Reach, southwest of Englishman's Bay; "Overflowed." *Vide* Moosepeckick and Moosabec.

Missiassick.

Missiassik, Abnaki village, Penobscot. H-B. of A-I. Vol. 1, p. 5.

Mkazaooktook, Little Black River, branch of the St. John and Pine Stream—a tributary of West Branch of Penobscot. "Black Stream."

Mobear? Island Pond, Cherryfield, Washington Co.

Moges Islands, Great and Little, Yarmouth, Cumberland Co.

Mohonon Branch, Cherryfield, Washington Co.

Molachenkamaeenk, one of Androscoggin Lakes.

Molechunkemunk Lake, Oxford Co.

Molly Ocket mountain, Woodstock, Oxford Co.; a corruption of Mary Agatha, who was the last of the Pequakets, and who died in Andover, Maine, in 1816.

Molunkus River, Benedicta, Aroostook Co; "a short stretch of high land on a small stream."

Molynuchgamog Lake, "a homely lake." Sockbasin.

Monagenest.

Monogenest, north side of St. John's River.

Monahigan Island, mouth of Penobscot. "Grand Island." Smith, 1614.

Monanis Bay, Pemaquid.

Monanis Isle, Pemaquid. Smith, 1614.

Monarda, Aroostook Co.

Monhegan Island, Lincoln Co. "Grand Island;" a corruption of Menahan.

Monhegan. *Vide* Monahigan, Morattigon, etc.

Monsapec, Jonesport.

Monseag, near Westport, "Place of island-waters."

Monsiocage Falls, near Damariscotta. M. H. S. Col.

Monsweag River, Wiscasset, Lincoln Co.

Monsweag Bay.

Montsweag, Woolwich, Sagadahoc Co.

Montagamon Lake, Penobscot River. *Vide* Mattagamon.

Montinicus. *Vide* Matinicus. H. H. Mass. Vol. 2, 132.

Mopang Lake and Stream, Cherryfield and Harrington, Washington Co.

Moosabec, the Reach, Jonesport. *Vide* Moosepeckick.

Moosebec, "Straits of a river." *Vide* Moosabec. Willis.

Moosebesic Pond, Mascamp, York Co.

Moosecajik, "Moose's rump." *Vide* Mosekachick.

Mooseckey, the Reach, Jonesport. *Vide* Moosabec.

Moose-horn Stream, Pemaquan Lake, Baring, Washington Co.

Mooseleuk Stream, a branch of the Aroostook; "moose place." L. L. H.

Mooselucmaguntic Lake, Oxford Co.

Mooselockmaguntic Lake. Willis.

Mooseelumaguntic, one of Androscoggin Lakes.

Mooselumaguntic Lake, Oxford Co.

Mooseetomaguntic Lake, Oxford Co. *Vide* Mooselucmaguntic. Willis.

Moosetookmeguntic Lake, Oxford Co; "where the hunters watch the moose by night."

Moose-parun, a name of Moosehead Lake, 1773.

Moosepeckick, West Machias; "overflowed." Same as Mispecky, q. v. L. L. H.

Moose Plantation, Somerset Co.

Moose River, Somerset Co.

Mootinoo, Isles of Shoals.

Mopang River, Washington Co.
Mopang Lake, Washington Co.

Morancey Pond, near Gouldsborough, Hancock Co.

Morattigon, same as Monhegan, q. v.

Mosekachick, Cape Rozier, Brookville, Hancock Co. "The Moose's rump." *Vide* Moosecajik.

Mashoquen, an Abnaki village on Maine Coast. Smith, 1616.

Moskwaswagamok, Shallow Lake, near Caucomgonoc. "Musk-rat lake." L. L. H.

Moskwaswagamocsis, Dagget Pond. Diminutive of preceding. L. L. H.

Mosquito Mountain? Franklin, Waldo Co.

Moteseniock Pond, Mattawamkeag.

Mountecaws, "York Records," XIII, p. 261.

Mountekee Neck, Arundel, York. "York Records," XIII, p. 678.
Mountequies Neck, Arundel, York. "York Records," XII, part 2, p. 265.

Mount Kineo, Moosehead Lake, Somerset Co.

Mount Scargery, Kennebunkport.
Mount Scargo, Kennebunkport.

Mousam River, Acton, York Co., formerly Cape Porpoise River, or Maguncook.

Mousam Pond, Acton, York Co.

Mousapec, Jonesport. *Vide* Moosabec.

Moxie River? Junction of Kennebec River.

Moxie Falls? Junction of Kennebec River.

Moxie Pond? Junction of Kennebec River.

Mskutook Lake, Schoodic, "Still water."   G.

Mskwamagweseeboo, Hale Brook, Penobscot. "Salmon Brook." L. L. H.

Mucalsea Mountain, Somerset Co.

Mundooscotook River, Sagadahoc : Kennebis resided at Swan Island, at the confluence of this river with the Kennebec.

Munolammonungun, west branch of Pleasant River, Piscataquis Co. "Very fine paint, or place where it is found."

Munsungun Lakes, head of Aroostook. "A cut;" "the fat of a bird;" "where they speared salmon," etc. L. L. H. Indefinite.

Munsungun River, Penobscot.

Munsungun Mountain, Grand Falls, Penobscot Co.

Muscongus Bay, Bremen, Lincoln Co.   Probably a corruption of

Muscongus Pond, Bremen, Lincoln Co.   Remobscus or Seremobscus.

Muscongus Island, Bristol, Lincoln Co.

Muscongus Sound, Bristol, Lincoln Co.

Muscongus Harbour, Bremen, Lincoln Co.

Musequoite, same as Maquoit. Boies, 1662.

Musquequoite, same as Maquoit. 1662.

Musquacook Lake, Allagash, "Birch-bark Place. ' L. L. H.

Musquash mountains, Talmage, Washington Co. "Muskrat."

Musquash Lake, West Talmage, Washington Co. "Muskrat."

Musquosh Cove. M. H. S. Col. 6, 2d, 139.

Muttonequis, Doucett's or St. Croix Island.

N

Naguncoth, near Wells, York. Suff. Records, 245, Vol. XI, 1649.

Nagwamqueeg, Mallison Falls, Presumpscot River. M. H. S. Col. 7, 2d 105.

Nagwasacke, Woolwich. 1639. *Vide* Nequasset.

Nahmajimskicongomoc, Haymock Lake, Allagash. "Lake of the dead-water that extends up into the high land." L. L. H.

Nahmakanta Lake and outlet, Penobscot, "where there are plenty of fish." L. L. H.

Nahsaick, Boyden's Lake, Washington Co.

Nahumkeag Island, Pittston, Kennebec Co., "eel-bed."

Nahumkeag Pond, Pittston, Kennebec Co.

Nahumkeeg. *Vide* Nahumkeag.

Nahumkeeg Falls, east side of Kennebec.

Nahumkeeg Island, east side of Kennebec. "Place where eels are taken." Willis.

Nahumkeeg Pond, east side of Kennebec.

Nahumkeeg Brook, east side of Kennebec.

Nalaseemagamobsis, Shad Pond, Penobscot. "Resting-place"— after poling up the river. L. L. H.

Nallahoodus, near Moosehead Lake, Penobscot, "a fall on each side." L. L. H.

Nallahootda, near Moosehead Lake, Penobscot. *Vide* Nulhedus.

Nallawagwis. *Vide* Narraguagus. "Something breaks that you cannot fix."   L. L. H.

Namadunkeeunk, Chester, Penobscot. "It goes up rapid from the mouth of the brook."   L. L. H.

Namahjimskitegwek, Smith Brook. "The dead-water extends into the high land."   L. L. H.

Namdamassuagum, Gardner's Lake, Washington Co.

Namokanak, same as Hockamock, q. v. "Highland—kind of a lump."   L. L. H.

Namscascock tract, Wells, York Co.   Suffolk Records, 245, Vol. XI, 1649.

Nampscascoke, Wells, York Co.   "York Records."

Nampscoscocke, Wells, York Co.   "York Records."

Nanhoc, a Tarratine river."   *The Sagadahoc Colony.*   Thayer, 89, 203.

Naquamke Falls.   *Vide* Nequamwick.

Narantsoak.   *Vide* Norridgewock.   Charlevoix.

Narraganset, Gorham.   "Maine Register."

Narragooe, Abnaki village.   *Purchas' Pilgrimage,* 1628.

Narraguagus River, Cherryfield, near Thomaston, Washington Co.

Narraguagus Bay.   "Something breaks that you cannot fix."

Narramissic, near Gardiner, Kennebec.   "Hard to find."

Nasahick Lake, Perry, Washington Co.   Hanson's *History of Gardiner.*

Nasgig Point.   M. H. S. Col. 6, 2d, 139.

Naskeag, Brooklin or Sedgwick, Hancock Co.

Naskeag Point.

Naskeigh.   M. H. S. Col. 4, 2d, 314.

Nasket Point, Woolwich, Sagadahoc. *Vide* Neskett and Nequosset.

Nauseag.

Naskege.

Nassaque. Smith, pp. 18, 20, 213, 214.

Natuah, an intervale. Hanson's *History of Gardiner*.

Naurantsouak, same as Norridgewock, q. v. *Vide* also Narantsoak. "Smooth water between rapids."

Nauseag. *Vide* Nasket.

Naxoat, St. John's River. H. H. Mass. Vol. II, p. 98.

Neaguamkot tract, Kennebec River. M. H. S. Col. 6, 2d, 400.

Necotok, same as Nicatou, q. v. West Branch of Penobscot.

Neccotoh, "where two streams meet," or "The forks."

Nechawonek River, Berwick, same as Newichawannock, q. v. "York Records," XIII, 751.

Neconaugamook, Round Pond, Washington Co.

Neddick Cape, York, York Co., same as Neddock, q. v.

Neddock Cape, York, York Co.

Negas, ancient Abnaki village on Penobscot River. H-B. of A-I. Vol. 1, p. 5.

Negewomicke River, near Dover. *Vide* Newichawannock.

Neghechewanck, same as Newichawannock, q. v. Wood's Map.

Negnankik Falls, Kennebec. *Vide* Nequamkik. "York Records," X, 176.

Negnomkag Island, Kennebec River. M. H. S. Col. 6, 2d, 401.

Negraugen, mouth of the Sheepscot River. "Our gateway." *Vide* Newagen.

Negunisis, "short falls and portage." G.

Neguasseag River, Woolwich, Sagadahoc Co. Deed, 1648.

Negunket River, between York and Wells. *Vide* Oguntiquit.

Negunticook, Camden, Knox Co., same as Megunticook, q. v.

Negusset, Woolwich, Sagadahoc Co. *Vide* Nequosset.

Negutaquit River, Kittery, York Co. "Old Eliot."

Neguttaquid River, Kittery, York Co. "Old Eliot."

Neguttaquid Marsh, Kittery, York Co. "Old Eliot."

Negutaquet, Kittery, York Co.

Negwasseg tract, between Sagadahoc and Sheepscot Rivers.
M. H. S. Col. 6, 2d, 401.

Nehumkeag Stream near Cobbosseecontee. "Eel-land." *Vide*
Nahumkeag.

Nehumkee Stream, near Cobbosseecontee. "Eel-land." H. H.
Mass. II, 418.

Nehumkike Stream, near Cobbosseecontee. "Eel-land."

Neihewonock River, Ossipee. M. H. S. Col. 4, 2d, 363.

Neketow, West Branch of Penobscot River. *Vide* Nicatou.

Nequamkeag, between Waterville and Augusta. *Vide* Nahumkeag. Willis.

Nequamkike.

Nequamkee tract, South Kennebec Co.

Nequamwick Falls, Kennebec. "York Records," Vol. IX, 169.

Nequamkik Falls, Kennebec.

Nequamkick Falls, Kennebec.

Nequaseag River, near Kennebec. "Clear-water place." *Vide*
Negusset, also Nequasset.

Nequaseg River, near Kennebec. "Clear-water place."

Nequassabem. "Large Pond."

Nequassabemacese. "Small Pond."

Nequasset, Woolwich, Lincoln Co. *Vide* Nequaseag.

Nequasset Pond, Woolwich, Lincoln Co.

Nequasset Creek, Arrowsick, Lincoln Co.

Nequosset, Woolwich, Lincoln Co.

Nequosset Pond, Woolwich, Lincoln Co.

Nerigwok, same as Norridgewock, q. v.

Neskett, coast from Penobscot Harbour to Mt. Desert. H. H. Mass. Vol. 2, 286, *note.*

Nesowadnehunk Stream, Katahdin. "The stream that rushes among the mountains." L. L. H.

Nesuntabunt mountain, near Nahmakanta. "Three-headed." L. L. H.

Newagen, Cape, Southport, Lincoln Co.; a corruption of Negraugen, q. v.

Newaggen, Cape.

Newichawannock, Berwick, York Co. "At the fork, or confluence of two rivers."

Nezinscot River, Buckfield, Oxford Co.

Nicatou, Medway, Penobscot Co. "The great forks."

Nickatous Lake, Hancock Co.

Nikaagamak, Ragged Lake, Chesuncook. "Upper Lake." L. L. H.

Noguncoth, same as Ogunquit, q. v. "York Records."

Nogunquet.

Nohikaimanahan, Deer Island, Moosehead Lake, translation of English : not original. L. L. H.

Nolangamoik, Ripogenus, Penobscot. "A resting-place" (after a long carry). L. L. H.

Nolatheeheemungun Island, old settlement. G.

Nollesemic, a Penobscot Lake; same as Nolangamoik.

Nollidgewanticook River. "River little interrupted by falls." Sockbasin.

Nollommussocongan Island, Penobscot River, "where they catch alewives." *L. L. H.*

Nolumbajik Pool. G.

Nolusokhungun Island, same as Nollommussocongan.

Nonesuch River? Scarborough, Cumberland Co.

Norridgewock, Madison, Somerset Co. Corrupted form of chief's name. "Smooth 'water between falls." "Place of deer?"

Norridgewock River, Madison, Somerset Co. "Smooth water."

Norridgewock River, Little, Chesterville, Franklin Co.

Norumbega, an ancient "country, city, and river said to have been discovered in the eastern part of U. S. by Verrazano, in 1524. The site has not been identified, although it is supposed to have been in the neighborhood of the Penobscot River, or Pemaquid.
Norumbegua.

Nosahick Pond, Perry, Washington Co.

Nubble Lake? Raymond, Cumberland Co.

Nuchawanak. *Vide* Newichawannock.

Nukacongamoc, Clear Pond. "Head-water Pond." L. L. H.

Nulhedus, a branch of the Penobscot. *Vide* Nallahoodus.

Numdemociss Stream, Washington Co. "Where the suckers go up to spawn."

Numtaceenaganawis, Elbow Lake, Penobscot. "A little cross pond." L. L. H.

Nuscongus, Bremen, Lincoln Co. *Vide* Muscongus and Nusconcus. Smith, 1616.
Nusconcus.

Nychioraunock River, near Piscataqua River. *Vide* Newicha-wannock. South Berwick. M. H. S. Col. Vol. 1, p. 340.

O

Oawasscoage River, Blue-point River, Scarborough. M. H. S. Col. Vol. 3, p. 27.

Obumkeag River. "York Records," Vol. 1, part, 2, p. 13.

Ogoncog River, corruption of Ogunquit, Wells. "York Records Vol. 1, part 2, p. 6.
Ogornog River.

Ogunquit, Wells, York Co.

Oguntiquit, ancient name of Negunket, q. v.

Okpaak, Abnaki village, H-B. of A-I. Vol. 1, p. 5.

Olamon, Abnaki village, Penobscot. H-B. of A-I. Vol. 1, p. 5.
Olamon Island, Greenbush, Penobscot Co.
Olamon Stream, Greenbush, Penobscot Co.

Olamman River, Penobscot River. "Paint place." G.
Olamman Island, Penobscot River. "Paint-place." G.

Olemon Island, Penobscot River, *Vide* Olamon.
Olemon Stream, Penobscot River.

Oloostook River, Aroostook. *Vide* Oolastook.

Onegla mountain. Willis.

Ongeachonta mountain, upper part of Kennebec.

Ooalaquemook, the Allagash River. "Black-camp River."

Oolagweskwigamicook (Allagaskwigamook)." Bark-cabin place."

Oolammonogamook, Silver Lake, K'taadn. "Vermillion-paint lake." L. L. H.

Oolastook, Aroostook. "Beautiful River."

Oosoola, South Norridgewock. "A spot frequently inundated."

Oquossoc. Rangeley.

Orampheagan, an arm of the Piscataqua, at Eliot, York Co.

Orantsoak, part of Kennebec River, same as Aransoak.

Orignal, Moosehead Lake.

Oriocoag River, Scarborough, Cumberland Co.

Orona, Penobscot Co.

Oroeskeag, aboriginal name of Dunstan. M. H. S. Col. 2d, Vol. IV.

Orqueachanta Mountains, Kennebec. Willis.

Osotonac Creek, Western Creek, Kittery. "York Records," XIV, 666.

Ossaghrage, Abnaki village. H-B. of A-I. Vol. 1, p. 5.

Ossipee River, Little, Acton, York Co. "Pine River," or "Stony River."

Ouwerage, Abnaki village. H-B. of A-I. Vol. 1, p. 5.

Ouygoudy, St. John's River.

Owascoag, Scarborough. "The place of much grass."

Oxygoudy, St. John's River. *Vide* Ouygoudy.

Ozwazogehsuck, Penobscot Brook. "When they carry by there they have to wade across 'quartering.'" L. L. H.

P

Paghhuntanuck, Abnaki village. Smith, pp. 18, 20, 213, 214.

Pagiscott. *Vide* Pejepscot. Mass. Bay Rec., Vol. 1, p. 272.

P'ahnmoiwadjo, Squaw mountain, Moosehead Lake. "What is of or belongs to woman." Not original. L. L. H.

Pamedecook Lake, Piscataquis Co. *Vide* Pemadumcook.

Pamedomcook Lake, Piscataquis Co. "Bar or shallow place between two lakes."

Pamgockamock Lake, "Muddy Lake," or "Bad Pond." *Vide* Pongonquamook.

Pamidumcook, one of Penobscot Lakes. "Lake of the sloping mountain," or "Muddy lake." *Vide* Pemadumcook.

Panahamsequet, same as Penobscot, q. v. Many variations. M. H. S. Col.

Panamske, Indian village at or near Oldham. *Vide* Pannowauske.

Panagamsde.

Panamouamke village, 1724. N. Y. Col. Doc. IX, 940.

Pananaushek, Penobscot River, about 1664.

Panawansot Hill, same as K'taadn, q. v.

Pannawanskek, Indian village at or near Oldham. *Vide* Pannowauske.

Pannowauske, Indian village at or near Oldham.

Pansagasewackeag, same as Passagassawakeag, q. v. M. H. S. Col.

Papootick, Falmouth, York. *Vide* Porpooduc and Papuduc.

Pappoose Pond, Albany, Oxford Co.

Papuduc, Falmouth, York.

Papuding, Falmouth, York.

Parmacheenee Lake, Rangeley system.

Parmacheenee Stream. *Vide* Appmoojenegamook.

Parmachene Lake, Oxford Co., same as Parmacheenee.

Pascodumoquonteag, same as Passamaquoddy, q. v. Willis.

Pascongamoc, Holeb Pond, Moose River. *Vide* Pescongamoc. "Branch of split lake."

Pasharanack, Abnaki village, 1616, "near the cove or bay." Gerard, H-B. of A-I. Vol. 1, p. 5.

Pashippscot, same as Pejepscot. M. H. S. Col. Vol, 1, pp. 75, 76.

Passadumkeag, Penobscot. "Beyond the sandy beach." Gerard. "Quick water." "Falls running over a gravelly bed." L. L. H. "Stream above falls." G.

Passagassawakeag Pond, Brooks, Waldo Co.

Passagassawakeag River, Belfast. Waldo Co. "The place of sights or ghosts."

Passamagamoc Lake and Rapids, Penobscot, a corruption of Pascongamoc.

Passamagammet.

Passamaquoddy River, Waldo Co. "From a word signifying 'pollock-fish,'" 'pollock-ground or haddock,' probably several species of fish." J. H. T.

Passamaquoddy Bay.

Passamacadie River. M. H. S. Col. 6, 2d, 226, 231.

Passataquack, said by some to be the original of Piscataqua. "Divided tidal-river place." *Vide* Proceed : Mass. H. S. 1878; also Smith, pp. 18, 20, 213, 214.

Passataquak.

Passumadeag River, Burlington, Penobscot Co.

Patagumpus Stream, tributary of Penobscot. "Sandy-ground cove."

Patagumkis Falls, Penobscot. "Half-circle point." G.

Patagumkis River, tributary of Penobscot. "Sandy-ground cove," or "a dry sandy place." L. L. H. *Vide* Patagumpus.

Pataquongamis, Telosinis Lake, Allagash. "Round Pond." L. L. H.

Patapso, "appointed place of meeting." Willis.

Pataweekongomoc, Telos Lake. "Burnt-land lake." L. L. H.

Pataweektook, Ragmuff stream, Penobscot. "Burnt-land stream." L. L. H.

Pattagumpus village, Penobscot Co.

Pattagumkis River, Medway, Penobscot Co. *Vide* Patagumkis.

Pattagussis, Smith Brook, Mattawamkeag.

Pattakumpis River, Medway, Penobscot Co. *Vide* Pattagumkis.

Pattaquonquomis Lake, Allagash River.

P'aytayweektook, Ragmuff Stream, Penobscot. "Burnt-ground stream."

P'tayweektook.

Pauhuntanuck, Abnaki village. *Vide* Paghhuntanuck.

Pechenegamook River, St. Francis' River. G.

Pechepscut. *Vide* Pejebscot.

Pechypscott. *Vide* Pejebscot (1690). Mather.

Peckwalket, same as Pegwacket, q. v. Sullivan.

Pedaugbiouk, head-waters of Damariscotta River. "The place of thunder."

Pedcokegowake.

Pedgodagowake, Sheepscot Co. Sullivan.

Pegwacket. *Vide* Pigwacket and Pequaket.

Pegwakick. *Vide* Pigwacket and Pequaket.

Pejebscot Falls, Androscoggin River.

Pejepscot, Brunswick, Androscoggin River.

Pegypscott, Brunswick, Androscoggin River. Sullivan.

Pemadumcook Lake, Piscataquis Co. "The place where the sand stretches through or across"—the lake. L. L. H. *Vide* Pamidumcook.

Pemaquan Lake, Charlotte, Washington Co.

Pemaquan River, Charlotte, Washington Co.

Pemaquid, Bristol, Lincoln Co. "At the place where the land slopes." J. H. T.

Pemaquid River, Bristol, Lincoln Co.

Pemaquid Ponds, Bristol, Lincoln Co.

Pemaquid Point, "Long point," or "that runs into the water."

Pemaquida, ancient name of Pemaquid. "Long point."

Pemaquideag, ancient name of Pemaquid. "Long point place."

Pematagoet River, Castine, Hancock Co. 1605. *Vide* Pentagoet.

Pemerogat.   M. H. S. Col. 7, 2d, 430.

Pemetic mountain, Mt. Desert, Hancock Co.

Pemetiq, Mt. Desert Island, E. Penobscot, "Sloping land." Father Biard. 1611.

Pemidumcook Lake, Penobscot River, "a gravel or sand bar runs through the middle of lake." *Vide* Pemadumcook.

Pemsquamkutook Island, Penobscot River. "Birch Island." G.

Pemtaquamktook, Penobscot River.   G.

Pemmaquan River, Pembroke, Penobscot Co.

Penjejawock River, Bangor.   *Vide* Pujejewock.

Pennemaquam village, Dennysville.   M. H. S. Col. Vol. 4.   Willis.

Pennamaquan, settlement, southeast of Dennysville, Eastport.

Pennamaquan River, Eastport.

Pennamaquan Lake, southeast of Dennysville, Eastport.

Pennamaquaon, Pembroke. "Maine Register."

Pennechuck. "York Records," XIV, 387.

Pennecoo Falls, Rumford. Willis.

Pennessewasse Pond, Great, Norway, Oxford Co.

Pennessewasse Pond, Little, Norway, Oxford Co.

Pennycook, Rumford Falls. *Vide* Pennecoo.

Penobsceag, Penobscot River. *Vide* Penobscot.

Penobskeag, Penobscot River. "A rocky place," or "place of rocks."

Penobscoote, Penobscot River.

Penobscot River, Penobscot Co. "Rocky place," "at the descending rock." J. H. T. "River of rocks."

Penobscot County.

Penobscot Bay.

Penobsquisumquisebou, Sandy River. Hanson's *History of Gardiner*, p. 20.

Penoomskeook=Penobscot River. "Rocky Falls." G.

Penopeauke=Penobscot River.

Pentacost Harbour? George's Island harbour.

Pentagoet Fort, Castine, Hancock Co. *Vide* Pematagoet.

Pentagoet Harbour, Castine, Hancock Co.

Pentagoet, Penobscot Bay.

Pentooskeag, same as Pentagoet. M. H. S. Col.

Pequaket, Fryeburg.

Pequaket, early name of Denmark, Oxford Co.

Pequawett, same as Pegwacket, q. v. Governor Lincoln.

Perpodack, Cape Elizabeth. *Vide* Porpooduck.

Pescongomoc, Holeb Pond, Moose River. "Branch or split lake." *Vide* Pascongamoc.

Peskebegat, Lobster Lake. "Branch of a dead-water," or "branching or split lake." L. L. H.

Peskebskitegwek, Soper Brook, Eagle Lake, Allagash. "Branch of a dead-water emptying into a lake." L. L. H.

Peskedopikeh, Alder Brook, west branch of Penobscot. "Branch of an alder-place." L. L. H.

Petcongomac, head of Allagash. "Crooked pond." L. L. H.

Pewagon, west branch of Pennamaquan River, Eastport. P. E. Vose.

Philamoosis River, Penobscot. "Little salmon stream." G.

Pichet mountain, Moss, Aroostook Co.

Pictou, Micmac village, N. S. Mass. H. S. Col. 1st, X, 116 (1809).

Pigwacket, Fryeburg. *Vide* Pequaket.

Pikaghenahik, Crooked Island, Penobscot River. "Curved or crooked island."

Piscasset stream. "White stone."

Piscataqua, Kittery, York Co.

Piscataqua River, Kittery, "Divided tidal-river." ("Dark or gloomy.") Aubrey.

Piscataqua Point, Kittery, York Co.

Piscataquack. *Vide* Passataquack.

Piscataquis River, empties into Penobscot. "Little divided tidal-river." "Little branch stream." L. L. H.

Piscataquis Co.

Piskataquis Lake.

Pnjejewock stream, Bangor, same as Penjejawock, q. v.

Pocamsus Lake, near Grand Lake, Washington Co.

Pockwockamus Lake, Penobscot. "Mud pond." L. L. H.

Pocopassum, Abnaki village. Smith, pp. 18, 20, 213, 214. 1614.

Pocumcus. Willis.

Pogomqua River, Casco Bay. *Vide* Pogumqua.

Pogopskekok stream, above Grand Falls. G.

Pogumqua River, Casco Bay. *Vide* Pogomqua.

Pohenagamook Lake.

Pohomoosh, Micmac village, N. S. Mass. H. S. Col. 1st, X, 116.

Pokey Lake, Crawford, Washington Co.

Pokumkeswagamoksis, Harrington Lake, Chesuncook, "a pond with a gravelly outlet." L. L. H.

Poland, Androscoggin Co., named for celebrated Indian chief.

Pongokwahem Lake, Allagash River.

Pongowakem Lake, "Heron Lake," Allagash. Willis.

Pongokwahemook, Eagle Lake, Allagash. "Woodpecker Place." L. L. H.

Pongonquamook, "muddy lake" or "bad pond." G.

Pongonquemis Lake, same as Pongonquamook. G.

Ponguongamook Lake, source of Allagash River, "muddy lake" (another name for Baamchenungamook). Named for Mohawk chief.

Popokomukwodchussu, Whetstone Falls, East Penobscot.

Porpooduck, Fore River, Cape Elizabeth. "A burying place." Ballard.

Possepscangamook, Cathance Lake, Washington Co. P. E. Vose.

Potawadjo, near Pamedumcook Lake. "Whale Mountain." L. L. H.

Potobek, Lily Bay, Moosehead Lake; "where the water bulges." L. L. H.

Pougohwakem Lake, Heron Lake, Allagash.

Pquakis "Red Pond." G.

Precaute, a village on Quibiquesson River, q. v. 1602.

Presumpscot village, Cumberland Co.

Presumpscot River, Falmouth, Cumberland, Co. "River of many shallows" or more probably from *ompsk*, "stone" and "*ut*" locative.   A-I. H-B. Vol. 2.

Presumpscot Falls, Falmouth, Cumberland Co.

Psiscontic, Brassua Lake, Moosehead; "handiest place to build canoes." L. L. H.

Psiscontic-Brassua, or Brassaway Lake, same as Psiscontic.

Puggummua Creek, Falmouth, Cumberland Co.

Pujejewock Stream, Bangor. *Vide* Penjejawock.

Pumgustuc, head of tide on Royall's River, North Yarmouth. *Pumgustuk.*

Pungustuc, Wescustogo, "York Records," Vol. 2.

Pushaw River, Oldtown, Penobscot Co.

Pushaw Lake, Oldtown, Penobscot Co.

Pushaw village, Oldtown, Penobscot Co.

Pushaw Pond, Oldtown, Penobscot Co. Willis.

Q

Quabacook, Merrymeeting Bay. "Duck-water place.?"

Quabeag Bay, north of Casco.

Quadotchquoik River. G.

Quagachusque, Devil's or D'Orville's Head.

Quaheag Bay, near Harpswell.

Quakis, one of Penobscot Lakes.

Quakish, same as Quakis, q. v.

Quakish, same as Quakis, q. v.

Quampheagen Falls, Salmon Falls River, South Berwick, York Co. "A place where fish are taken in nets." Sullivan. *Vide* N. H.

Quampiasan landing, in old town of Kittery, South Berwick. **Quampiaysan.**

Quamscook, one of Cobbesecontee Ponds.

Quanoscomcook, St. Andrews, Eastport.

Quantabagood Pond. M. H. S. Col. 7, 2d, 198.

Quantecook Lake, near Belfast.

Quassabam Island. "Pond Island," G.

Quawcohead. M. H. S. Col. 6, 2d, 139.

Quentabacook Pond, Searsmont, Waldo Co.: source of St. George's River.

Quesquitcumegee, Warren. Willis.

Quesquitcumegek Ridge, between Thomaston and Westkeag River. "High carrying place."

Quibiquesson River, "in Bashaba's dominions," near Pemaquid *Purchas' Pilgrimage,* Lond. ed. 1673, 74.

Quinnebequi, early name of Kennebec. "Long still water."

Quisquamago ridge, between Thomaston and Westkeag River. "High carrying place." Willis. *Vide* Quesquitcumegek.

Quito Hill, Casco, Cumberland Co.

Quoddy Head, at Lubec, Washington Co.

Quohog Bay, near Harpswell.

R

Ramassoc, a village on the Penobscot. *Purchas' Pilgrimage,* 1628.

Rascohegan, name of Georgetown, Sagadahoc Co.

Rasthegon Island, Sagadahoc.

Remobscey. "York Records."
Remobscus. Vide Muscongus.

Reskeagan Island (probably ancient island). *Vide* Rascohegan.

Ripogenas River.
Rippogenus, one of Penobscot Lakes.

Rocameca, an Abnaki village. H-B. of A-I. Vol. 1, p. 5.

Roccamecco, Jay Point. Indian Planting-ground.

Rockabema Lake, Moro, Aroostook Co.

Rockomeko Point, at Canton, Oxford Co.
Rockomeko Mountains, Canton, Oxford Co.

Romomeko, East Livermore, Androscoggin Co. "Great corn-
land."

Roswic, same as Arrowsick, q. v.   Reed's *History of Bath,* 1804.
Rowsick.
Rowsik.

Rumfeekhungus? Place near Bath where there was a school for
Indians in 1786.   Reed, *opus cit.*

S

Sabada Pond, New Gloucester. M. H. S. Col. 8, 2d, 279.

Sabatis Hill. *Vide* Sabatos,

Sabatos mountain, named for an Indian who accompanied
Arnold's expedition.

Sabbatus Lake, Androscoggin Co.

Sabbatus Mountain, Androscoggin Co.

Sabino, Phipsburg, Sagadahoc. 1608.

Sabino, near mouth of Sagadahoc River; so-called for a Sagamore of that name.

Sabotawan, the eastern of Spencer mountains. "The end of the pack"—where the strap and buckle are. L. L. H.

Sacadiock. *Vide* Sagadahoc.

Sacantry, Cape, Kennebec River. M. H. S. Col. 6, 2d, 400.

Sacarabig, on Presumpscot. "Toward the rising sun." *Vide* Saccarappa. Willis.

Sacasawakie River, Morrill, Waldo Co.

Saccarappa village, at Westbrook, Cumberland Co. "Toward the rising sun."

Sacatyhock. *Vide* Sagadahoc. B. Church's *History of Indian Wars*, p. 201.

Sackatehock. *Vide* Sagadahoc.

Saco, York Co. Derived from Shawakatoc, or Shawocotuck, a tribe residing there. *Vide* Sawocotuck.

Saco River, York Co.

Saco Bay, York Co. It may mean "the outlet," or "outflow"— literally "a pouring out."

Sagadahoc River, Kennebec River. "Land at the mouth," or "mouth of the river."

Sagadahoc Co.

Sagadahock.

Sagadonoc.

Saghibpatook Falls, near Chesuncook. "Rough, or hard, falls." L. L. H.

Sagosset Island, Sagadahoc. *Vide* Chegoney.

Sahbimskitegwek, Thoroughfare Brook; "a stream that empties between two large bodies of water." L. L. H.

Sahkhabehaluck, Moose River, Moosehead Lake. "There is more water flowing from it than from any other stream that empties into the lake." L. L. H.

Sahkkahegan, Telos Lake; "water connecting with another body of water." L. L. H.

Salko Hill, near East Machias, Washington Co.

Salquin Island, ancient name for Sutquin or Sequin, q. v.

Sankderank. *Vide* Sunkataradunk. Willis.

Sankderand, near Pemaquid. M. H. S. Col. 2d, Vol. 4, 289.

Sapompeag, same as Lapompeag, q. v. "rope," or "crooked stream."

Saponic Pond, Burlington, Penobscot Co. *Vide* Suponic.

Saquasis-diggin Island, Casco Bay. "York Records" XII, 2d part, p. 261. *Vide* Sebascodegan.

Sasana, ancient by-river near Boothbay Harbor.

Sasanoa River, Kennebec River. Willis.

Satquin. *Vide* Sutquin. Smith, 1616.

Saugus Island, Penobscot River. "Bad Island." G.

Sawacook, north side of Pejepscot, Topsham.

Sawacotoc, ancient name of Saco River. *Vide* Saco, Willis and Prince.

Sawocotuck, ancient name of Saco River. Prince.

Sawahquatook, ancient name of Saco River. Smith.

Sawguatock, ancient name of Saco River. M. H. S. Col.

Sawadabscook. *Vide* Sowadabscook.

Sawkhead, same as Sawquid and Sunkeath, q. v. *Annals of Warren*, C. Eaton, p. 21.

Sawquid, Pleasant Point, Cushing. Willis.

Scaggrock River? tributary of Mattawamkeag, Orient, Aroostook Co.

Scargery mountain, Kennebunkport, York Co.

Scargo mountain, Kennebunkport, York Co.

Scataway hill, Scarborough, Cumberland Co.

Scatuck, Indian form for Schoodic River.

Scoodeag River, St. Croix. "Front River," or "low, swampy meadow."

Scoodeag Lakes. Gallatin says that, in the Passamaquoddy dialect, it means "burnt land."

Schoodic River, Passamaquoddy Bay; "where fish live all the year."

Schoodic Lakes, Passamaquoddy Bay. *Vide* Scoodeag.

Schoodic, several lakes and streams in Maine. "Burnt lands, or "Trout place."

Schoodiac Pond, at Cherryfield, Washington Co.

Scitterygusset. *Vide* Squitregusset and Squidrayset.

Scouhegan Falls, Kennebec River.

Sebacook. *Vide* Sebec. G.

Sebago Lake, Bridgeton, Cumberland Co. "Great water;" "a stretch of water." "To vomit." J. G. C.

Sebaik, Abnaki village, Passamaquoddy. *Vide* Sebec. "River crossing."

Sebamook, Abnaki name for Moosehead Lake. "Extending water."

Sebasco Island, Casco Bay. *Vide* Sebascodegan.

Sebascodegan Island, Harpswell, Cumberland Co. *Vide* Sebascodiggin.

Sebascodiggin, Great or Orr's Island, Harpswell, Cumberland Co.

Sebascohegan River, a tributary of Mattawamkeag.

Sebasticook, Benton, Kennebec Co.
Sebasticook River, Benton, Kennebec Co.

Seebaticook, Indian Pond, Kennebec River. "'Logon' stream."
L. L. H.

Sebaycook. *Vide* Sebago.

Sebec Lake, Bowerbank, Piscataquis Co. "Bright, or extending water."
Sebec Lake, Barnard, Piscataquis Co.

Seboeis Lake, Penobscot Co. *Vide* Seboois.
Seboeis Stream.
Seboeis Plantation.

Seboois River, branch of Penobscot; "a brook or small stream :" "*Little river*."
Seboois Lakes, Aroostook Co.

Seboomook, Elm stream, on the Penobscot.

Secarabigg Falls, Amancongon River.

Seeboycook, Passamaquoddy, same as Sybaik, q. v. "Pleasant point."

Segeunkedunk stream, Brewer, Penobscot Co.

Segochet, ancient name for St. George's River. Smith, 1616.
Segocket.

Segochet, Thomaston, Knox Co. Abnaki village, 1614.
Segohquet, St. George's River. *Vide* Segochet.
Segotago, Abnaki village. H-B. of A-I. Vol. 1, p. 5.
Seguin Island, near Monhegan, Lincoln Co. *Vide* Sutquin.
Segumkedunk River, Brewer. Willis.

Semiamis headland, near Cape Elizabeth. *Sagadahoc Colony*, Thayer, p. 69, 70.

Senaglecouna, early northern boundary of Maine, "a great wood."

Sennebec Lake, at Union, Knox Co.

Seremobscus River, east of Pemaquid. *Vide* Muscongus.

Shawacotoc, early name of Saco River.

Shawakatoc, the name of a tribe formerly residing where Saco now is.

Shawocotuck.

Shebeag. *Vide* Chebeague.

Shecoway River, Casco Bay. *Vide* Skeecoway.

Sheepscot River, Georgetown, Sagadahoc Co. "Little bird place." or "Bird-flocking river."

Shepscooke River.

Shippscutt River.

Shohomagock's Hill, near Dover.

Sisquisic, Cousin's River, North Yarmouth. *Vide* Sysquissett.

Skeecoway River, Casco. "York Records," Vol. 1, p. 134.

Skitacook Lake, Oakfield, Aroostook Co.

Skitticook River, branch of Mattawamkeag. "Dead-water stream."

Skowhegan, on the Kennebec.

Skowhegan Falls, on the Kennebec. *Vide* Scouhegan.

Skutarza, a form of Eskutassis, q. v.

Skukoal Island, Grass Island. G.

Soadabscook Stream, Etna, Penobscot Co.; "a place of large, smooth rocks." *Vide* Sowadabscook.

Sobscook, Nichol's Rock, Penobscot River. "In the river at the head of the tide." G.

Socatean stream, flowing into Moosehead Lake. "Standing Atean" from name of brave chief; or "half burnt land, and burnt timber."

Sockhigones, ancient name of Saco River. Gorges.

Soghali-manahan, Sugar Island, Moosehead Lake : merely an English-Indian rendering of Sugar-Island.

Sologismoodik, Five-island Falls. G.

Songo River, Portland.
Songo Pond.

Sooneybec Pond, "Shady place." Willis.
Sooneybeag Pond, "Shady place." Willis.

Souneunk Stream. "That runs between mountains. "

Sourdnabunk Lake, Piscataquis Co.
Sourdnahunk Lake, West branch of Penobscot.

Sowadabscook, branch of Lower Penobscot; "a place of large, smooth rocks." L. L. H. *Vide* Sawadabscook.

Sowadapscoo, Indian form of Sowadabscook. General Herrick.

Sowhigginock. "York Records," XIV, 387.

Sowocatuck, Sokoki village, Saco River. Smith, 1616.

Sowungun Island, Eagle Island. G.

Spurwink River, Cape Elizabeth, Cumberland Co. H. H. Mass., 1, 311.

Spurwinck River, Cape Elizabeth, Cumberland Co.

Squa-pan, at Masardis, Aroostook Co.

Squamokweeseeboo stream, Penobscot. "Little Salmon stream." G.

Squattack Lake, near northern boundary of Maine.

Squaw Heights, at Westport, Lincoln Co.

Squaw Mountain, Moosehead Lake. "The mountain which belongs to a woman?"

Squaw Island, White Island, Greenbush, Penobscot Co.

Squaw-pan Lake, Castle-hill, Aroostook Co.

Squethequinset Creek, Casco Bay. "York Records," XII, 2d part, p. 357.

Squidrayset Creek, at mouth of Presumpscot River : name derived from chief.

Squiddera Gusset Creek, at mouth of Presumpscot River. "York Records," XIII, p. 377.

Squitheragusset Brook. *Vide* Squidrayset.

Squitregusset Creek, at mouth of Presumpscot River. *Vide* Squidrayset.

Squittergussett's Creek. "York Records," XIII, p. 613.

Subecwangamook, Hadley's Lake, Washington Co.

Sugalmanahan, Penobscot River, Sugar Island. *Vide* Soghalimanahan.

Suncook, early name of Lovell, Oxford Co.

Sunkaradunk, mouth of Kennebec River. "Kennebec Claims."

Sunkataradunk, ancient name of Sagadahoc. "Mouth of Rivers." Sewall.

Sunkatunkarunk, Sagadahoc. *Vide* Sunkataradunk.

Sunkeath, same as Sawkhead, q. v.

Sunkhaze stream, Greenfield, Penobscot Co. "Dead-water at the mouth"— of the stream.

Suponic Pond, Burlington, Penobscot Co.

Susquesong, Cousin's Island, North Yarmouth.

Susgussugg, Cousin's Island, North Yarmouth. "York Records," VIII, 233. *Vide* Susquesong.

Sutquin, Sequin Island.   *Vide* Salquin, Satquin and Sequin.

Swackadock, between Cape Elizabeth and Cape Porpoise.   "York Records," XIV, 299.

Swagadahock, Kennebec River (Saco River).   Willis.

Swanckadocke River, Saco River.

Swegustagoe River, Royall's River.   *Vide* Wecustego.

Swome tract, Kennebec River.   M. H. S. Col. 6, 2d, 400.

Sybaik, Pleasant Point, Passamaquoddy, same as Sebaik and Sebec, q. v.

Sysquisset Creek, North Yarmouth.

Sysladobsis Lake, near Grand Lake, Washington Co.   "Rocky lake."   L. L. H.
Sisladobsis.

T

Tacook, near Oldtown.   "Waves."   L. L. H.

Taconnet, Waterville, Somerset Co., "a place to cross."   Hanson's *History of Gardiner.*

Tacconnet Falls, Waterville, Somerset Co.

Tahanock, St. George's River.   Simancas Map, 1610.

Tallagodissik River, Webster's Island.   "Painting place for squaws."   G.

Taplino? Taplins Island, Damariscotta Bay.

Taughtanakagnet.   Smith p. 18, 20, 213. 214.

Teconnet.   *Vide* Taconnet.

Telastinis Lake, south of Chamberlain Lake.   Willis.

Telos Lake, near Webster Lake.   *Vide* Pataweekongomoc.

Telosinis Lake, south of Chamberlain Lake.   *Vide* Pataquongamis.

Temahkwecook, Aroostook Co. "Beaver Place." L. L. H.

Temisconata Lake, near northern boundary of Maine. Williamson.

Tepenegine, south of Sheepscot River. M. H. S. Col. 6, 2d, 401.

Tewissicke, same as Capisic, q. v.

Ticonic Falls, Waterville, Somerset Co. *Vide* Taconnet.

Tiowawaye, Third Lake, East Penobscot. L. L. H.

Tirsick. M. H. S. Col. 6, 2d, 401.

Tobique, Abnaki village (Maliseet). H-B. of A-I. Vol. 1, p. 5.

Togus River, Augusta.

Togus Lakes, Augusta.

Togus, Augusta.

Tokanock Falls, Kennebec River. M. H. S. Col. 6, 2d, 401.

Tolam, Indian name of ancient Falmouth. De Laet, 1633.

Tomah River, Waite, Washington Co.

Tomah Pond, Waite, Washington Co.

Tomah Mountain, Codyville, Washington Co.

Tomah, Little Stream, Codyville, Washington Co.

Tomahegan Pond, Tomhegan Pond, Moosehead Lake. "An axe or hatchet." A corruption.

Tombegewoc, Deering Pond, Salmon Falls River, Sanford. Lydston grant.

Tomhegan, near Moosehead Lake, Somerset Co.; evidently not original.

Tonnemony Hill, York.

Tonquewac, one of the summits of Russell mountains, Somerset Co.

Totononnock, Waterville, Somerset Co.

Toulbah mountains. "A turtle."

Towrook, early name of Lebanon. M. H. S. Col. 6, 2d, 306.

Towwoh, early names of Lebanon, York Co.
Towow.

Tuladi River, near northern boundary of Maine. Williamson.

Tulamdie River. *Vide* Tuladi.

Tulandic River, branch of Upper St. John. "Where they make
canoes." L. L. H.

Tunk, Big Mountain, Cherryfield, Washington Co.
Tunk, Young Mountain, Cherryfield, Washington Co.
Tunk, Great and Little Pond, Cherryfield, Washington Co.
Tunk Stream, Cherryfield, Washington Co.

U

Ulmsasket Ponds. *Vide* Umsaskis. G.

Umasaskis, Sausage Lake, Allagash River. "Tied together like
a sausage."

Umbagog Lake, Oxford Co. "Clear, shallow lake."

Umbazookskus. *Vide* Umbazooskus.

Umbazookscus, Penobscot, "meadow-place." Willis.

Umbazooskus, one of Penobscot Lakes, "meadow-place."

Umcoleus Lake, near Aroostook River.
Umcoleus Stream.

Umcolquis. *Vide* Umcoleus. Derived from a word signifying
"whistling duck."

Umquolcus River, Oxbow, Aroostook River.

Umsaskis Lake, on Allagash. "Tied together like sausages,"—having opposite points which run out to meet one another. L. L. H.

Unsuntabunt, Rainbow Lake. "Wet head;" probably corruption of Nesuntabunt.

Unyjaware, Abnaki village. H-B. of A-I. Vol. 1, p. 5.

Upquedopscook, Fish River, entering St. John's.

Upquedopsk River, entering St. John's. "Fish River," same as Upquedopscook. G.

Usgha River. Willis.

V

Viger, Abnaki village (Maliseet). H-B. of A-I. Vol. 1, p. 5.

W

Wabacosoos Lake. Willis.

Wabacosoas Lake. M. H. S. Col. Vol. 4, p. 111.

Wabasses Lake, near Grand Lake.

Wabenungteekook, Penobscot. "Crooked Falls." G.

Wabiggamus, Abnaki village, Penobscot River. Smith, pp. 18, 20, 213, 214.

Wabossagock, Liberty Point, Robbinston. P. E. Vose.

Waccago, Abnaki village. *Vide* Wakcogo. Smith, pp. 18, 20, 213, 214. 1614.

Wahkasekhoc, on Mattawamkeag River. "Where moosehide frames were left, after the hides had been cut out." L. L. H.

Wakcogo, Abnaki village, same as Waccago.   Smith, *opus cit.*

Wakeag, same as Waukeag (Sullivan,)q. v.

Waksrong, Kennebec River.   M. H. S. Col. 6, 2d, 401.

Walumpkuas River.   G.

Wallagrass Lakes, at Eagle Lake, Aroostook Co.

Wallahgasquegamook, Back Wigwam Lake.   G.

Wallangasquegamook Lake.   G.

Wallastook, St. John's River.   L. L. H.

Wallenipteweekek, South Twin-lake, Penobscot.   "Round coves surrounded by burnt land."

Walloostook River, St. John's River.   *Vide* Wallastook.   "Stream where you get smooth boughs;" or "Beautiful River."   L.L.H.

Wapskehagan Mountain, Baileyville, Washington Co.

Wapskenegan River, Alexander, Washington Co., same as Wapskehagan, q. v.

Waquaick, Oak Bay, Eastport.   P. E. Vose.

Warbeggamus.   *Vide* Wabiggamus.   Smith, *opus cit.*

Wasaumkeag, Stockton, Waldo Co.

Wassataquoick Mountain, one of Katahdin range.   *Vide* Wassategwewick.

Wassataquoick River, eastern branch of Penobscot.   *Vide* Wassategwewick.

Wassategwewick, eastern branch of Penobscot.   "Place where they spear fish;" or "Place of the bright or sparkling stream."   L. L. H.

Wassatiquoick, same as Wassataquoick.   Willis.

Wassoosumpsquehemok Island, Marsh's Island, Penobscot.   G.

Wassumkedewadjo, White-cap mountain, K'taadn; "white-sand mountain."   L. L. H.

Watchig Pond, Great, at Standish, Cumberland Co.

Watchig Pond, Little, at Standish, Cumberland Co.

Watoolwagamook, St. John Pond. "Pond where you keep cattle, sheep, caribou, moose, etc."—"good hunting-ground." L.L.H.

Waukeag, Sullivan, Hancock Co. "A seal."

Waunnakeseag, "place of mackerel." Willis.

Wawenock, probably Woolwich, Sagadahoc Co. *Vide* Mowhotiwormet Proper Names.

Wawrigwick, same as Norridgewock, q. v. Smith, 1616.

Webhannet, Indian name for Wells, York Co. when it included Kennebunk.

Welokenabacook Lake, Oxford Co.

Welokinbacook, one of Androscoggin Lakes.

Wennigansege tract, mentioned in deed of Robinhood, May 29th, 1660,—usually known as the Gutch deed.

Wenniganseye River. *Vide* Winnegance.

Wescogus, Pleasant River, Columbia, Washington Co.

Wescustogo, North Yarmouth, Cumberland Co. Royall's River. *Vide* Swegustagoe.

Wessamesskek River, Westkeag. *Vide* Wessawasskeag.

Wessanansit River, near Skowhegan. M. H. S. Col.

Wessanensit River, Skowhegan. Willis.

Wessawasskeag, Westkeag, "a land of wonders." To show how the old Indian names degenerate, this name was contracted to Westkeag by the first settlers, afterwards to Keag, and finally to "Gig," the modern appellation.

Wessaweskeag, Thomaston. "Land of sights." Willis. *Vide* Wessawasskeag.

Wesserunset, former name of Canaan, Somerset Co.

Wesserunset River, at Brighton, Somerset Co.

Wesserunsicke, same as Wesserunset, q. v.

Westecustego, same as Wescustogo, q. v.

Westkeag River, South Thomaston, Knox Co.   *Vide* Wessawass-keag.

Weweautit.   Vose, Dennysville.

Wewenoc, Abnaki village, Pentecost Harbour.

Whichacasecke, same as Wiscasset, q. v. "York Records," vol. 2.

Whisgeag.

Whisgeag stream, Bath, Sagadahoc Co., "rapidly running water."

Whisgig, near Bath, same as Whisgeag.

Whizgeag, near Bath, same as Whisgeag.

Whiskeag, near Bath.

White-Squaw Island? Greenbush, Penobscot Co.

Widipidlock River, Mattawamkeag.   *Vide* Wydopidlock, etc.

Willimantic, Dover, Foxcroft, Piscataquis Co.

Wincittico River, Sheepscot River. "York Records," XII, 2d part, p. 367.

Wincittico Falls, Sheepscot River, "York Records," XII, 2d part, p. 367.

Winganssek.   *Vide* Wennigansege.

Winnaganset, Boothbay.

Winnecook Lake, Unity.

Winnegance Village, Sagadahoc Co.   *Vide* Winneganseek.

Winnegance Creek, Phipsburg, Sagadahoc Co.

Winnegance Stream, Bath. "A river boundary of lands."

Winneganne, near Pemaquid, "carrying place."

Winneganseek. *Vide* Wennigansege.

Winnegangseag carrying-place, near Pemaquid, Sagadahoc Co.

Winnigans. *Vide* Wennigansege.

Winscheag Bay, east of Mount Desert.

Wiscasset, early name of Dresden, Lincoln Co.

Wiscasset, Sheepscot.

Wishcassick, in New Dartmouth. *Vide* Wiscasset.

Wissacasset. *Vide* Wiscasset.

Withee? Dover, Piscataquis Co.

Woboostook, Baker Stream, St. John River. "The waters appear white." L. L. H.

Wolomontegus Stream, Pittstown, Kennebec Co.

Wombemando Island, Penobscot River. "White-man's Island." G.

Woolastaququam Hill, Aroostook Co.

Woolastook, St. John River. *Vide* Wallastook. "Stream where you get smooth boughs," or "Beautiful River."

Woolastookwaguamok, Baker Lake. "Lake of the stream where you get smooth boughs." L. L. H.

Woolastaquaquam, preceding name as applied to stream from lake. L. L. H.

Worumbo, at Lisbon, Aroostook Co.

Woromontagus River, Augusta, Kennebec Co.

Worromontogus River, Augusta, Kennebec Co.

Wydopidlock,
Wydopiklock, branch of Mattawamkeag. "The river is broad, and there are no trees on its banks except alders." L. L. H.
Wytopidlot.
Wytopitlock Lake, Mattawamkeag.

X

Xsebem, early name for Moosehead Lake. "Bright water;" or "Extending water." L. L. H.

Y

Yeapskesset, Wells, York Co. "York Records," 1, part 2, p. 11.

NEW HAMPSHIRE

Agiocochook, White Mountains.   Belknap.

Ahquedaukee, The Wiers, Winnipesaukee.

Ahquedaukenash.   *Vide* Aquedoctan.

Amenonoosuc River, west tributary of Androscoggin River.
Ammoosuc River.

Ameriscoggin River, Coös Co., former name of Androscoggin.

Ammonoosuc River, Upper, Carroll Co., branch of Androscoggin.
   "The small or narrow fishing-river."

Ammonoosuc River, Lower, flows into Connecticut River.

Amokeag Falls.   Same as Amoskeag, q. v.

Amokeag Village.   Same as Amoskeag, q. v. "Fishing-place."

Amoskeag Falls, in Merrimack River.   "One takes small fish."
   H-B. of A-I.   Vol. 1, p. 50.

Androscoggin.   *Vide* Ameriscoggin (also Androscoggin, Me.)

Annahooksett Falls, Suncook.

Aquahatan, Winnipesaukee, where head of Merrimack River is-
   sues out of lake.

Appalachia Station, in Randolph.

Aquedaukenash, same as Ahquedaukenash, q. v.   "The Weirs."
Aquedoctan.
Aquedahtan.

Ashaeolock.   *Vide* Ashuelot.

Ashuelot River, Cheshire Co. "Collection of many waters."

Ashuelot, former name of territory now known as Keene and Swanzey.

Ashuelot Pond, in Washington.

Ashuelot Mountain, in Winchester.

Ashuelot Station, in Winchester.

Ashuelot, Upper. *Vide* Ashwillet.

Ashwillet River, Cheshire Co. Same as Ashuelot, q. v.

Asquam Lake, Holderness, Grafton and Carroll.

Asquam Mountain, Holderness, Grafton and Carroll.

Asquam River, Holderness, Grafton and Carroll.

Asquamchumauke, former name of Baker's River in Grafton Co.

Asqueanunckon Brook, mentioned in India   ed, 1683. 19. N. H. State Papers, 358.

Attilah, Peak of White Mountains. "Blueberries."

Attitash Mountain, in Bartlett.

Awososwi Menahan Island, Winnipesaukee Lake. "Bear Island."

B

Babboosic Lake. Station in Amherst; same as Papoosuc.

Baboosuc Pond, in Amherst and Merrimack.

Baboosuc Brook, in Merrimack. Papoose (Baby) Brook.

Baboosuc Brook, Little, Hillsborough Co.

Babboosuck. Winthrop.

Bold Sunapee Mountain, in Newbury. *Vide* Sunapee.

C

Cabassauk, early name of Merrimack River. "Place of the Sturgeon."

Cabbo Lake, in Windham. Fox's *History of Dunstable.* Map facing p. 13.

Catamount Pond, Little Pond, Boscawen.

Chebeaque, (Geebig Road), near North River, Dover. Name derived from that of an Indian Chief. *Vide* Jebucto.

Chickwalnipy River, in Coös Co.

Chickwolnepy River, in Coös Co.

Chickwalnipy Mountain, in Milan and Success.

Chocorua Lake, in Tamworth.

Chocorua Mountain in Albany. Mountain named from Indian killed on summit by hunters, in time of peace.

Chocurua, Ossipee, Carrol Co.

Chocurua Peak, Mount Washington Range.

Cocheco, present form of name of Dover.

Cochecha, Dover. Deed 1673. *Vide* Thompson's "Landmarks," p. 255.

Cochchechoe River, 1648.

Cochecho.

Cochechoe, Great Hill, Dover, 1652. *Vide* Thompson's "Landmarks," p. 89.

Cochecho Point, Dover.

Cochecho Marsh, Dover.

Cocheco Pond, in Dover and Somersworth.

Cochecho River and Falls, in Strafford Co.

Cohas Brook, in Manchester. "Little pine-tree."

Cohos, same as Coös.

Connecticut River. "Long tidal-river."
Connecticut Lake, in Pittsburg, N. H.

Contoocook, former name of Boscawen. "Crow place or River."
Contoocook River, in Merrimack and Hillsborough Counties.

Coös County, (diminutive of Coa). "Pine-tree." "Place of
  pines." Same as Coasset, Mass. This is an Indian name, although, curiously enough, it occurs in the New Testament.

Coosuc Village, mouth of Lower Ammonoosuc. "At the pines."
  Vide Coassitt, Mass.

Cowissewaschook, Indian name for Kearsarge Mountain "Proud
  or selfish one" J. G. C. "Pointed or peaked mountain." J. H. T.
  Vide plan of Andover, 27 N. H. State Papers, 86–87.

Cusumpe Pond, original name of Asquam Lake, q. v.

D

Duncanowitt, former name of hills in Dumbarton. Hammond.

G

Gaentake, former name of Beaver Brook, in Windham.
Gonic Village, in Rochester.   *Vide* Squamanagonick.

H

Husow tract, near Madbury.   *Vide* Whisow, and Whisone.
Husone tract, near Madbury.   *Vide* Whisow, and Whisone.

Hyponeco Brook, in Swanzey.

J

Jebucto. *Vide* Chebeaque, (Geebig Road), Dover. Name derived from that of Indian who lived near North River. Thompson's "Landmarks," p. 82.

K

Kancamagus Mountain, in Livermore. Derived from name of Indian chief.

Kaskaashadi, early name of Merrimack River. "The place of broken water."

Kchi Pontegok, Somersworth, Strafford Co. "At the great falls."

Kearsarge Mountain, between Sutton and Salisbury. There has been much discussion as to the derivation of this name, many contending as to whether it is of Indian origin or not. If Indian, it must be an Abnaki word, and an Abnaki authority defines it as meaning "The proud or selfish one." On the other hand, Dr. Trumbull's definition is "Pointed or peaked mountain," and Dr. Potter favours "High place." *Vide* Cowissewaschook.

Kecheachy, original Indian name for Cocheco (Dover). Stevens, 1833.

Kinnicum Pond in Candia.

Kodaak Wadjo, Mount Washington. "The top is so hidden,"— in the clouds.

Kuncanowet Hills, Dunbarton. "Bear-Mountain place."

L

Little Babboosic Pond, in Amherst. *Vide* Babboosic.

Little Monadnock Mountain, in Fitzwilliam and Troy. *Vide* Monadnock.

Little Squam Lake, in Holderness and Ashland.   *Vide* Squam.

Little Sunapee Lake, in New London.   *Vide* Sunapee.

Little Suncook River, in Epsom.   *Vide* Suncook.

M

Magalloway River, Coös Co.   Doubt has been expressed as to this name being aboriginal.

Magalloway River, Pittsburg.

Magalloway Mountain, Pittsburg.   *Vide* Margallaway.

Maharimutts Hill, Hicks's Hill, Madbury.

Mahermits Hill, Hicks's Hill, Madbury.

Mahomet's Hill, Hicks's Hill, Madbury.   *Vide* Moharimet.

Malagoe River, northeast branch of Bellamy River, Barrington.

Mallego River, northeast branch of Bellamy River, Barrington.

Malamake River, same as Merrimack, 1685.   Letter of Kancamagus, S. G. D. p. 297.

Margallaway.   *Vide* Magalloway, (a tributary of Androscoggin.)

Mascoma Lake, Enfield.   "Place of the Bear?"

Mascoma River, Grafton Co.

Mascoma Pond, Dorchester.

Mashamee River, near Canaan, Grafton.   M. H. S. Col.

Masheshattuck Hill, in Pelham.

Masquane Lake.   *Vide* Mascoma.   "Birch-bark lake."   J. G. C.

Massabesic Lake, in Manchester and Auburn.   "At the great lake."

Massassecum Pond, in Bedford.   Named from Penacook Indian.   *History of Warner*, p. 29.

Mattabeesick Pond, Chester, Rockingham Co. "At the great, or large, lake or pond."

Mattabesec. *Vide* Massabesic.

Menunquatucke, Gilford. *Vide* Conn.

Merramacke, same as Merrimack, q. v.

Merrimack River (old Abnaki). "Deep or profound river;" J. G. C., or "swift water."

Merrimack Co.

Merrimack Town.

Minnesquam Lake, in Holderness, near Asquam.

Minnewawa River, in Cheshire Co.

Moharmot's Hill, Hicks's Hill, Madbury.

Moharimet's Planting-ground, near Lamprey River, Durham. These various names are evidently corruptions from that of an Indian Chief, called Mahomet, who lived in the neighborhood during the XVIIth Century (1686). *Vide* Thompson's "Landmarks," p. 150. *Vide* Maharrimutts.

Moharimet's Hill

Moharimet's Marsh.

Mohermitis Hill.

Mohawk River, in Coös Co.

Molnichwock Brook, in Errol and Cambridge.

Monadnock Mountain, in Jaffrey and Dublin.

Monadnock Lake, Dublin. "At the silver mountain," or "Place of the unexcelled mountain."

Moniack, early name of mouth of Merrimack River. "Place of the Islands."

Monnomake, same as Merrimack, q. v.

Monomack, same as Merrimack, q. v.   H. H. Mass. 2, 343.

Monomonock Lake, in Rindge. Name transferred from land. May mean either "Island Place," or "watch, or look-out place." *Vide* Wonomonock.

Montinicus, near Portsmouth.

Mossilauke Mountain, Benton. *Vide* Moosilauke.

Moosilauke Mountain, in Benton. "Bald place?"

Moosilauke Brook, in Woodstock.

Munt Hill, Hampton Falls. Named from an Indian who frequented the place. *History of Hampton Falls,* p. 387.

N

Naacook. *Vide* Naticook.

Naamhok. *Vide* Namaske.

Nacook Brook, "east of Merrimack River." J. G. D. *Vide* Naticook.

Naimkeak. *Vide* Namaske.

Namaske, same as Amoskeag, q. v. "At the fish-place."

Namaoskeag, same as Amoskeag,

Naumkeag, same as Amoskeag, "eel-land." J. H. T.

Naimkeak, same as Amoskeag.

Naamhok, early name of Amoskeag.

Namaskeag.

Namaoskeag. *Vide* Namaske.

Narmarcungawack River, in Coös Co.

Narragansett, former name of territory of Amherst, Goffstown, and Bedford.

Nashua City, in Hillsborough Co.

Nashua River, in Hillsborough Co. "Between." "Land between."

Natahook, 1695.

Naticook Brook, in Merrimack, former name of part of Litch-field.

Natticook.

Natukkog, Letter 1685.

Natukko, S. G. D. p. 297. "A cleared place." C. E. Potter. "History of Manchester." p. 27.

Naumkeag. *Vide* Namaske, also Naumkeag, Mass.

Nechawonack, same as Newichwannock, q. v. 1720. Thompson's "Landmarks," 104.

Nechewannick. Deed 1661. Thompson's "Landmarks," 104.

Nechowanuck River, near Salmon Falls, 1691, Thompson's "Landmarks," 74.

Nichewanok River, 1722. Thompson's "Landmarks," 103.

Negewonnick. Deed, 1619. Thompson's "Landmarks," 156.

Negewonnuck. *Vide* Newichwannock.

Newichwannock River in Strafford Co., former name of territory about Dover.

Newichawannock River, Strafford Co.

Newichawannock, Piscataqua (Kittery), "my wigwam place." Jenness, *First Planting of N. H.*, p. 56.

Nesenkeag Falls, Merrimack River, between Merrimack and Litchfield ; later, called Cromwell's Falls.

Nessenkeag Brook, Great, Litchfield.

Nesssenkeag Brook, Litchfield.

Nichiquiwanick. *Vide* Newichwannock. Maverick's MS. 1660. "my wigwam place." J. S. Jenness.

Nichewane. *Vide* Newichwannock.

Nichmug River.   Grafton Co.

Nippo Pond, near Isinglass River, Lamprey River, Dover.

Nissitisset River, Hillsborough Co.

Nissitissett, former name of territory about Hollis.

Nomascom.   Lebanon.

Norwottock, former name of locality in Hudson and vicinity.

Nubanusit River, in Peterborough and Harrisville.

Nubanusit Lake, in Hancock and Nelson.

O

Opechee Lake, between Gilford and Laconia; known also as
   Round Bay.

Osceola Mountain, in Waterville.

Ossipee Lake, in Ossipee and Freedom. "A lake formed by an
   enlargement of the river."

Ossipee town, in Carroll Co.

Ossipee Mountain, Carroll Co.

Ossipee River, Carroll Co.

Otternic Pond, in Hudson.

P

Pack Monadnock mountain, in Temple and Peterborough. *Vide*
   Monadnock.

Pannaway, original name of settlement at Little Harbour.

Pannukog, Concord 1685. *Vide* Penacook. "Crooked river, or
   place."

Pannukhog, Concord.

Papposuc, Amherst, a brook or pond.

Papoosuc, Amherst. *Vide* Baboosuc.

Parmachene Lake, in Coös Co.

Pascassick River, Rockingham Co. *Vide* Washuck and Watchic.

Pascassokes River, Gorge's Patent, 1631. *Vide* Piscassick.

Pascataquack, former name of Great Bay, between Durham and Newington.

Pascaquack.

Pascatoquack, near Smith Isles (now Isles of Shoals), same as Piscataqua, q. v. "Young Pilgrims." 351.

Pasquaney Lake, Newfound Lake, Bristol.

Passaconaway Mountain, in Waterville. Named for great sachem of Pennacook Indians.

Patuckaway mountains, White mountains' range.

Paugus Mountain, in Albany.

Paugus Lake, between Gilford and Laconia; known as Long Bay.

Pawtuckaway River, in Rockingham Co.

Pawtuckaway Pond, in Nottingham.

Pemigewasset River, in Grafton Co., "swift or rapid current," or "crooked place of pines."

Pemigewasset Pond, in Meredith.

Pemigewasset Mountain, in Lincoln.

Pemmemittequonitt Pond, in or near Pelham.

Penacook, former name of Concord. "Crooked river, or place," or "At the bottom of the hill or high land." Gerard.

Pennacook, former name of Concord. "Crooked river, or place," or "At the bottom of the hill or high land." Gerard.

Penacook Lake, in Concord.

Penagooge, Concord, 1675. *Vide* Penacook.

Pennichuck Brook, between Nashua and Merrimack.
Pennichuck Pond, in Hollis. Name transferred. "Crooked place."
Pennechuck Brook. Suffolk Rec. 449, vol. IV.

Pequawket, former name of region about Conway. "Crooked place."
Pequawket River, in Carrol Co.
Pequawket Pond, in Conway.
Pequawket Mountain, in Bartlett and Chatham.
Pequaket River, Conway.
Pequawkett, said to have been original form.
Pequaknet.
Pegwagget. *Vide* Pigwacket and Pickwocket.

Pickwocket. *Vide* Pequawket.   Sullivan.
Pigwacket. Belknap.

Piscassick River, Rockingham Co.   Indian name of Lamprey River.
Pissacassick River, "White Stone." *Vide* Piscasset, Maine.

Piscataqua River, Rockingham Co.; former name of Portsmouth. "Dark or gloomy river," Father Aubrey. "The confluence of two rivers."

Piscataquog River, in Hillsborough Co.
Piscataquog Mountain, in Lyndeborough.
Piscataquog village, an ancient Indian settlement, former name of West Manchester, now abbreviated to "Squog."

Piscataway River, Odiorne's Point, Little Harbour. *Vide* Piscataqua.
Pissacassick River. *Vide* Piscasset. "White Stone."

Plausawa, mountain in Pembroke and Chichester.   Named from Indian. *History of Pembroke*, 1.

Ponemah, in Amherst.

Pontoocook Bay or Cove, in Androscoggin River, at Dummer.

Potanipo Pond, in Brookline.

Potanopa Pond, in Brookline.

Powwow River, Kingston.

Puscassick. *Vide* Piscasset.

Q

Quampeagin, Deed, 1728. Thompson's "Landmarks," p. 213. *Quamphegan* Falls, at Somersworth.

Quamscott Falls, Exeter. *Vide* Squamscott.

Quocheco, Dover, Strafford Co. *Vide* Cochecho.

Quocheco River, Strafford Co.   *Vide* Cochecho.

Quomphegan Falls, Deed, 1652. Thompson's "Landmarks," p. 79.

Quonektacut River, Connecticut River. "On long river."

Quoquinnapasskessanahnog, former name of locality in Amherst.

Quoqunnapassackessanahhoy tract, Suffolk Rec. 449, Vol. IV.

S

Saco River, in Carroll Co. "From the south side." J. G. C. "Outlet." J. H. T.

Saco Falls.

Sagamore Creek, in Portsmouth.

Sagumskuffe, former name of locality in Nashua.

Scatawit, Dover. *Vide* Thompson's "Landmarks," p. 46.

Scatnet, in Dover City. *Vide* Thompson's "Landmarks," p. 229.

Scatuate, Dover. *Vide* Thompson's "Landmarks," p. 45.

Schohomogomock, former name of hill in Rochester. Suff. Rec., 215, Vol. XII, 1679.

Schoodac Brook, in Warner.

Sementels, Salmon Falls, Strafford, "gravel, or grains of rock."

Seminenal River, Salmon Falls River, "grains of rock." J. G. C.

Shadogee, Madbury. Probably not Indian. May be a corruption of Châteaugay?

Shatagee.

Shankhassick, former name of Oyster River, in Rockingham Co. *Vide* Thompson, *opus cit.*, p. 232. See also Sunkhaze, Maine.

Shoneeto, former name of Beaver Pond, in Derry.

Ska' ıtahkee Hill, in Hancock.

Sonoogawnock River, Coös Co. *Vide* Souheganock.

Soucook River, in Merrimack Co., former name of Israel's River, Coös Co. "Stony River," or "at the rocks." J. G. C.

Souheganack River, Souhegan, Hillsborough Co.

Souheganock, later Souhegan river, in Hillsborough Co., former name of Peterborough, Bedford and Amherst. "At the pointed river." J. G. C.

Souhegan, same as Skowhegan, Maine. "Pointed, or south, opening." "Entering inlet to south river." J. G. C.

Souhegan West, Amherst.

Souhegan East, Bedford.

Squam River, in Ashland.

Squam Lake, in Grafton and Carroll Cos. *Vide* Asquam.

Squam Mountain, in Holderness. This name is an abbreviation of Asquam—"Pleasant water place."

Squammagonic, near Dover, on Cocheco River. Probably "a salmon fishing-place." J. H. T.

Squannagonick Falls.

Squammagonake, old planting-field, near Dover, 1686.

Squamanagonic Falls, Rochester, Cocheco River.

Squamonagonic, Deed 1734, Thompson's "Landmarks," p. 237.

Squommonygonnock, Deed 1743, Thompson's "Landmarks."

Squamanagonic village, Rochester. *Vide* Gonic. "Water from the clay-place Hill." *Vide* Thompson, p. 61.

Squamscot, former name of Exeter and vicinity.

Squamscot River, in Rockingham Co. *Vide* Squamscott.

Squamscott Falls, Exeter.

Squamscott, Exeter.

Squamscott River, in Rockingham Co. *Vide* Squamscot.

Squannicock, tributary of Nashua River.

Squomscutt, Exeter. Winthrop.

Sunapee Lake, between Merrimack and Sullivan Cos.

Sunapee Mountain, in Newbury.

Sunapee town, in Sullivan Co., named for lake. "Stone Lake." J. G. C.

Suncook River, in Merrimack and Belknap Cos.

Suncook village, in Pembroke, and Mountain in Belknap Co.

Suncook Pond, in Northwood.

Suncook Pond, in Barnstead, former name of Pembroke. "At the rocks." J. G. C.

T

Tanipus Pond, same as Potanipo, Hillsborough Co. "Cold pond."

Tecumseh Mountain, in Waterville.

U

Umbagog, partly in Maine, in Errol and Cambridge also. "Clear lake," "doubled up," "shallow," or "great waters near another!"

Umpammonoosick, former name of Oliverian Brook, Grafton Co. Hammond.

Uncanoonuc Mountain, Hillsborough Co. "Breasts."

Uncanoonucks Mountain, Hillsborough Co. "Breasts."

W

Wachipauka Pond, in Warren, otherwise Meader Pond.

Wainooset. *Vide* Mass. H. H. Mass. 1, 407.

Wampineauk, on Merrimack River. "Place of clear water."

Wankewan Lake, in Meredith and New Hampton.

Waukewan.

Wanosha Mountain, in Thornton.

Wantastquet Mountain, in Chesterfield, Cheshire Co.

Wantastiquit Mountain, in Chesterfield, Cheshire Co.

Wantestiquet Mountain, in Chesterfield, Cheshire Co. *Vide* Wantastiquet River, Vermont.

Washuck River, same as Piscassick, q. v.

Washucke, land between Piscassick and Lamprey Rivers.

Washuck Neck, between Piscassick and Lamprey Rivers.

Watahook Mountain, same as Watatic, q. v.

Watchit River, same as Washuck, q. v.

Watchet Neck, same as Washuck, q. v.

Watchick River, same as Washuck, q. v.

Watananock, Nashua River. "Land about the hill," derived from land. J. H. T.

Wataqua, original name of Nashua River. "Pickerel." J. G. C.

Watatic Mountain, in New Ipswich.

Watahook Mountain, in New Ipswich.

Wettetook Mountain, in New Ipswich.

Wateticke Mountain, in New Ipswich.

Waternomee Mountain, in Woodstock Named from Indian chief.

Waterquechee Falls, in Connecticut River, at Plainfield.

Waterqueechy.

Wateticke. *Vide* Wataqua.

Wattannanuck, former name of hill, in Hudson. *Vide* Watananock.

Wattanummon Hill, near Manchester.

Wattanummon's Brook, Concord. Named from chief.

Waumbec, contraction of Waumbekketmethna. "White water."

Waumbek.

Waumbekket, contraction of Waumbekketmethna, q. v.

Waumbekketmethna. "The white mountains."

Wawobadenik. "At the white mountains."

Wecanacohunt. *Vide* Wecohamet. Hilton's Patent, 1629–30.

Wecohamet, Hilton's Point, Dover or Northam; Stevens, 1833. H. H. Mass. 1, 99.

Weekasoak, former name of Brook, in Nashua.

Weetamoo Mountain, Campton. *Vide* Weetamoo—"Proper Names."

Wequash, or Wickwas Brook, in Meredith.

Wequash Pond, in Meredith. *Vide* Wequash—in "Proper Names."

Wettetook. *Vide* Watatic.

Whisone tract, near Madbury. *Vide* Husow and Husone.

Whisow tract, near Madbury. Deed, 1693, Thompson's "Landmarks," p. 271.

Whrisone tract, near Madbury. Deed, 1702, Thompson's "Landmarks," p. 271. *Vide* Wisrisow.

Winicowett, Hampton. *Vide* Winnicut and Winnecowett.

Winichahanat, same as Wecohamet, q. v.

Winichahanant, same as Wecohamet, q. v.

Winichahauat, same as Wecohamet, q. v.

Winnecowett, former name of Hampton. "Beautiful place of pines."

Winnicunnet.

Winnepauket Lake, in Webster.

Winnepesaukee Lake, in Belknap and Carroll Cos.

Winnepesaukee* River, in Belknap Co. "Good water-discharge," originally applied to the outlet, J. H. T. — or "Lake region," or "region of Lakes." J. G. C.

---

*Appended to this chapter is a most interesting collection of the various modes of spelling of the name Winnepesaukee (as found, after a laborious search among "the records, maps, gazetteers, and general history of the state") by Mr. Otis G. Hammond, of the State Library, N. H. One hundred and thirty-two verbal forms are given, evidencing only too clearly the processes of mutilation and corruption to which the aboriginal names have been subjected by their transcribers.

Winnicot River, in Rockingham Co., former name of Stratham.
Winnicot Falls, in Rockingham Co.
Winnicut, in Rockingham Co. "Beautiful place."

Winnicouett, tributary of Piscataqua. *Vide* Winnicot.

Winnichahannat. *Vide* Wecohamet.

Winnisquam Lake, in Belknap Co. "Pleasant water."

Winona, in New Hampton.

Wisconemuck Pond.

Wisrisow. *Vide* Whisow.

Wonolancet Mountain, in Albany. *Vide* "Proper Names."
Wonalancet Mountain, in Albany.

Wonomonock. *Vide* Monomonock.

NEW HAMPSHIRE'S LARGEST LAKE AND ITS ORTHOGRAPHY.*

By Otis G. Hammond,† Esq. M. A.

Another outing season has come and with it come the usual throngs of summer visitors to pass their short vacations around New Hampshire's largest lake; but of all those who will gaze in admiration over its island-dotted surface, at the blue mountains of the north country, or cast a line in the vain attempt to land the largest trout of the season, how many will know how to spell the curious old name the Indians have handed down to us?

I have often heard it said that there were nineteen different ways of spelling the word, which, according to Chandler E. Potter, New Hampshire's best authority on Indian history and nomenclature, means "the

* Republished by permission.
† Assistant Editor of State Papers, N. H.

beautiful water of the high place," and is made up from *winne* (beautiful), *nipe* (water), *kees* (high), and *auke* (place). It occurred to me one day to prove the truth or falsity of such a statement, and, from that time forth, I sought and recorded every form of the name that I could find in the course of my work among the manuscript and printed records of my native state. The result was startling, and seemed to indicate that no other word or name in New Hampshire, certainly, and possibly in all New England, is capable of being spelled, or rather mis-spelled in so many different ways. Instead of the beggarly number of nineteen, I found one hundred and thirty-two, and my field was confined to the state and provincial records, maps, gazetteers, laws, and works on the general history of the state. If one should search the records of the towns in the vicinity of the lake the number might be doubled and possibly more. Spelling was not a strong point with our forefathers, and the unconscious ingenuity of ignorance produces wonderful results with a few letters. The clearing of spaces in the wilderness for houses, and the struggle with the earth for the actual necessities of life, left little time for mental culture. School facilities were few, and book-learning was left to the minister and the "squire."

The saying in regard to the nineteen different forms I think must have originated from a foot-note by John Farmer in his edition of "Belknap's History of New Hampshire," page 56, in which he notes eighteen forms besides the one ordinarily in use. Following are the one hundred and thirty-two spellings which I have collected, and I am quite sure the reader will find no two of them alike. A search for two like forms he will find as interesting and confusing as "Pigs in clover." These are all actually found either in manuscript records or print, and not one of them is the result of the writer's imagination:

Winnipiseokee	Winnepisioco	Winnipissiocky
Winepiseoka	Winnepissiacoe	Wenapesioche
Winnipisseake	Winnipistioky	Winnapissiaukee
Winnepesaket	Winispisiokee	Winnepissocay
Winepesocky	Winnepiseoke	Winnapuseakit
Winnepesocket	Winnipesokie	Wennepisseoka
Winnipisseoce	Winnepesiokee	Winipisinket
Winnepesaot	Winnapresseakit	Winipisiackit
Winnepisiokee	Winepisseokie	Winnepiseogee
Winnipeseoke	Winnepisseokie	Winnepisseogee
Winnipishiokee	Winipisioke	Winnepiseoge
Winepissiocke	Winipisioky	Winnipesaukee
Winipissiokee	Winassosawque	Winnipesocee
Winnipisiocke	Winipisaro	Wenepesocke
Winipissiockee	Winepessockey	Winnipissiackee
Winipiseocee	Winnespiseoky	Winneposockey

Winipisiocke

Winnepisseoke

Winnepossoke

Winnipissokee

Winnipissiokee

Winnepiseokee

Winnipisioke

Winipisiokee

Winnepesockee

Winnipisiokee

Winnipissioke

Winnepissk

Winnipesse

Winepessiockee

Winnepissiokee

Winnipissioca

Winipissioca

Winnipisseoccee

Winnipisseoce

Winnipiseoce

Winipishokee

Winnipeshokee

Winnipesauke

Winnepesauke

Winnipissaoke

Winnapusseakit

Winnepesaukee

Winipasekek

Winepiscocheag

Winnipissiockee

Winnepissioke

Winnipessioke

Winnipissauky

Winnipicioket

Winnipaseket

Winnapissaacka

Winnepissaocoe

Winnipishokey

Winnisposiokee

Winnispisiokee

Winnipoisekek

Winipoisekek

Winnepeseochee

Winnepisseogg

Winniposockett

Wenepesiokee

Wennepesiokee

Winnepeseochee

Winipesocee

Winepisackey

Winepisokey

Winnepiseoky

Wenepesioca

Winisipisiokie

Winnipissacca

Winnipisocy

Winneposssockey

Winnepisseohcee

Winipissikee

Winnepescocco

Winipisokee

Winnepisseockegee

Winnepasioke

Winnepissiaukee

Winnepesiaukee

Winnipesocket

Winipisseoca

Winipisiakit

Winnipiseogee

Winipiseogee

Winipissioket

Nikisipique

Winnipesaukay

Winnepiscockee

Winnipissiocki

Winepossockey

Winnipishoky

Winnipisokee

Winnepishoky

Winnipiseoca

Winnepsackey

Winipesoakey

Winnopisseag

Wenepesiocho

The presence of the double "n" and the final double "e," and the possible doubling of the "s" are responsible for many variations, and the contest between the terminations "auke" and "eogee" for many more. John Farmer, in his foot-note before mentioned, says the word "was probably pronounced Win-ne-pis-se-ock-ee." If the Indian gave the name six syllables it is an argument for the ending "eogee," but the present generation has shortened it to five, and the tendency of the last few years is in favor of "auke" with another "e" added. The latter form is generally given as the white man's representation in letters of the sound the red man made when he meant "place." The same sound may be represented by other letters, of course, and the difference between "auke" and "eogee" is very slight, beyond that represented by "k" in one and hard "g" in the other.

A few citations to works using the different forms will best show the great confusion that has existed for a hundred years in regard to the correct spelling,—

Winnipiseogee is used in "Barstow's History of New Hampshire," both editions, 1842 and 1853; "Sanborn's History of New Hampshire," 1875; "Merrill's New Hampshire Gazetteer," 1817; "Whiton's History of New Hampshire," 1834, index, the form in the text being Winnepiseogee; "Index to Council Records," 1631–1784, pub. 1896; "General Statutes," 1867.

Winnipiseogee, "Belknap's History of New Hampshire," three editions, 1784, 1792, 1813.

Winnipissiokee, Holland's map of New Hampshire, 1784, and here it is also called Richmond; map of New Hampshire, by Samuel Lewis, 1794, in Carey's General Atlas, 1795.

Winnepissiokee, "New Hampshire Laws," 1805.

Winnepisiogee, "Farmer and Moore's Gazatteer of New Hampshire," 1823; "Farmer and Moore's Historical Collections."

Winnepissiogee, "Carter's Geography of New Hampshire," 1831.

Winnepiseogee, "Zell's Atlas," 1875.

Winipissioket, "Map of the most Inhabited Part of New England," etc., engraved by Thomas Jefferys, London, 1755.

Winnipisiokee, Blanchard and Langdon's "Accurate Map of his Majesty's Province of New Hampshire in New England," etc., Portsmouth, October, 21, 1761, engraved by Thomas Jefferys.

Nikisipique, Emanuel Bowen's "New and Accurate Map of New Jersey, Pennsylvania, New York, and New England," etc., London, 1752.

Winnipesaukee, "Hurd's Atlas of New Hampshire," 1892; "Public Statutes," 1891; "General Laws," 1878; "House and Senate Journal," 1895; Calvert's *Weirs Times;* "Report of Endicott Rock Commissioners," 1892; and reports of other commissioners to the house of representatives in 1879 and 1883.

Winnepesaukee, "Index to New Hampshire Laws," 1886; "Potter's History of Manchester, N. H.," 1856.

Winnipissiogee, "New Hampshire Laws," 1815 and 1830.

Our own state officials have never been able to fix on any particular form of spelling, if we may judge by the state publications, as may be seen by the differences in the various compilations of laws   The same state of affairs exists in the law reports.   The most recent public prints seem to favor the form Winnipesaukee, and it is to be hoped that this or some other of the one hundred and thirty-two may hereafter be used to the exclusion of all others.   Any *one*, even the fantastic Nikisipique, would be better than all of them.   But when doctors disagree every man will decide for himself.

VERMONT

Algonquin Mountain. Warren.

Ascutney Mountain, Windsor. "Fire mountain," or "Three brothers," from three valleys: it may be a corruption of *Cascadnac*, "a peaked mountain with steep sides." Kendall.

Azzasataquake, early name of Missique River. "The stream that turns back."

B

Bomoseen Lake, Castleton, Rutland Co. "Pleasant water."
Bombazine Lake, Castleton, Rutland Co. "Pleasant water."

Belamaqueen Bay, Ferrisburgh. Lake Champlain.
Bellamaqueam Bay, near St. Albans.

Bopquam Bay, Swanton.
Bulwagga Bay, opposite Addison.

C

Canaghsione, Ticonderoga, N. Y.

Caniaderi-Guaranti, early Iroquois name of Lake Champlain. "The Gate of the Country."

Caughnawaga, near Sorel River, a name also applied to the Indians of Quebec.

Chippenhook? Spring, Rutland.
Chippenhook? Village, Rutland.

Cohasse. *Vide* Coös (Newbury). "Little pine-tree."

Coös, name of Newbury, 1789. "Pine tree."

Coosuck, Ox Bow, Newbury.

E

Ekwanok Mountain, Manchester, Bennington: now known as Equinox. Dr. S. A. Green.

Elligo Scootlon Lake, Greensborough and Craftsbury.

H

Hoosac River, Pownal, "mountain rock."

Hoosic River, Pownal.

Hinkam? Pond, Sudbury.

I

Iroquoisia, earliest name of Vermont.

K

Kahshahquahna, Whitehall.

Kakiconte River, Boscawen.

M

Magog River, flows into Memphremagog Lake.

Magog Lake. *Vide* Memphremagog.

Manickmung Mountain, Stratton.

Maquam Bay, Swanton. A corruption of Bopquam, q. v.

Maquam Lake, Franklin Co.

Massawippi Lake, Holland.

Matincook, Leamington.

Memphremagog Lake, Orleans Co. "Beautiful water," or "Lake of abundance."

Mettawee River, Dorset. *Vide* Pawlet.

Michiscoui River. *Vide* Missiquoi.
Michiscoui Bay.

Mink Brook, Concord.

Missique, a corruption of Masseepsque. "The place of arrow flints."
Missique Bay, Alburgh.

Missisco River, Lowell.
Missisco, a corruption of Missikisko,—"much waterfowl."

Missisquoi River, Orleans Co. "Big woman?"
Missisquoi village (early).
Missisquoi Bay.

Moosalamoo, Lake Dunmore, Salisbury.

Musquash meadow, near Harriman's Brook, Newbury.

N

Neshobe, Brandon, Dorset.
Nickwackett.
Nulhegan River, Averill and Wenlock.
Nulhegan Pond, Bloomfield.

O

Ompompanoosuc River, Vershire.

Otta Quechee Falls, Windsor Co. *Vide* Quechee. "Quick, whirling falls."

Ouynouske Bay, Mallet's Bay. Earliest name of Winooski, q v.

P

Paran? Creek, Shaftesbury.

Passumpsic River, or Moose River, Caledonia Co. (Concord), "much clear water."

Passumpsic village, Caledonia Co.

Pawict.

Pawlet River, Dorset. *Vide* Mettawee.

Pecunktuk Stream, Great Otter Creek. "Crooked river."

Petoubouque, Lake Champlain. (Abnaki). "The waters that lie between,"—the countries of the Abnaki and the Iroquois. According to John Watso or Wadhso, an intelligent Indian of St. François.

Pico Peak, Clarendon.

Pompanoosuc, West Norwich, Windsor Co.

Poousoomsuck River, rises at Westmore.

Popasquash Island, near St. Albans.

Popoquamanutuk, Au Sable River. "The Cranberry River."

Q

Queechee River, Windsor Co.
Quechee River.

Quechee Falls. *Vide* Otta Queechee.
Quechee Valley.

S

Sadawga Pond, Whitingham; probably named for local Indian of same name.

Sancoik, near Bennington.

Saranac River, a corruption of Senhalenactuk,—"the river of sumach trees." Franklin Co., N. Y.; flows into Lake Champlain.

Schaghiticok, name of Indian tribe, and of their residence.

Schuytook.

Shatterack mountain, Jamaica.

Squamkeag, formerly in Vermont. *Vide* Skuakheag, and Squakeag, Mass.

Sungahneetuk, Lewis Creek. "The Fishing-river."

T

Tickenecket Pond.

Tickeneck Pond.

Ticklenaked.

Tsinondrosie, Ticonderoga, N. Y. "Noisy or rushing water."

W

Walumscoick River, Bennington. *Vide* Walloomsac.

Walloomsack, Bennington. *Vide* Walloomschaick.

Walloomsack River, Bennington.

Walloomscaik River, Bennington.

Walloomschaick River, branch of Hoosac River, Bennington.

Wanascatok Brook, Broad Brook, Vernon. "River of otters." *Vide* Wonakaketuk.

Wantastiquet River, West River, Weston, Windsor Co.

Wantastitquck River, West River, Weston, Windsor Co.

Wicopee Hill, Dummerston.

Winooski River, Cabot, near Burlington. "Beautiful River." Name transferred from land. (Abnaki).

Winooski Falls, Cabot.

Winooski Gorge, Cabot.

Winooski Village, Cabot.

Winoosque, early spelling of Winooski.

Wonakaketuk Stream, Little otter. "River of otters." *Vide* Wanascatok.

LIST OF THE PRINCIPAL AMERICAN-INDIAN TRIBES, REPRESENTING THE ABORIGINES OF NEW ENGLAND

Aberginians, a term used by the Massachusetts settlers to designate the Indian tribes to the northward. H-B. A-I. Vol. 1, p. 1.

Abnaki or Abenaqui,—"men of the east" or "Eastland." They constituted an Algonquian confederacy centered in the state of Maine which subsequently overflowed into the northern section of New Hampshire. They are said to have consisted, linguistically, of all the tribes occupying the East or Northeast shore of America. The term was first applied to the Indians of Nova Scotia. They occupied mainly the whole of the country between the Piscataqua and Penobscot rivers. *Vide* Introduction.

Agawams. The word Agawam is said to mean "a fishing station" or "fish-curing place." Two or three places in Mass. were so-called; the Indians resident at Wareham, Plymouth Co. were Wampanoags, in 1620— and those living at Ipswich, in Essex Co. (probably Mass. Indians or Nipmucks) at the same time, were both known as Agawams.

Algonkins or Algonquians, were the most widely extended of all North Americans Indians, their territory stretching along the Atlantic coast from Labrador to Pamlico Sound and westward from Newfoundland to the Rocky mountains. Their various tribes, linguistically affiliated, spoke innumerable dialects. The meaning of the word is "on the other side" (of the river), or "at the place of spearing eels, and other fish,"—from the bow of canoe. H-B. A-I. Vol ., p. 38.

Amoskeags or Namaoskeags (Nipmucks of New Hampshire) were situated at the Amoskeag Falls on the Merrimack, in the vicinity of Manchester. The name has been defined as meaning the term "a fishing place for alewives."

Anasagunticooks or Arosagunticooks. This tribe was a branch of the Abnaki nation and dwelt about the sources of the Androscoggin river.

Armouchiquois. *Vide* Malecites.

Aucociscos, a branch of the Abnaki. They occupied territory between Saco and the Androscoggin river. The meaning of is given as signifying "a crane "or "a heron."

Canibas. *Vide* Kanibas.

Etchemin. This tribe is now considered to have been a sub-group of the Abnaki confederacy, speaking the same language, but a different dialect and to have included the Passamaquoddy and Malecite. They are said to have extended from the Penobscot to the St. Croix river as far as St. John. Later they resided in the neighborhood of Passamaquoddy river. The meaning of the term has been interpreted as "Canoe-men."

Hammonassets, a tribe in Connecticut, resided in the neighborbood of Clinton and Killingworth. Sebequanash, or "The man who weeps," was their head sachem.

Hassanamissits, a tribe of Nipmucks, occupied the site of Grafton, Mass.; they embraced Christianity in 1660.

Kanibas, a branch of the Abnaki, who occupied both sides of the Kennebec river, Maine.

Machemoodus, a small tribe, probably a fragment of the Wangunks, situated near East Haddam, Conn. Much superstition prevailed among them owing to mysterious noises proceeding from the adjacent hill known as "Mount Tom," and here the Indians, as an early writer says:—"drove a prodigious trade at worshipping the devil!"

Mahicans, Mohicanders or Monahiganeucks, an Algonquian tribe extending from Esopus to Albany on the banks of the Hudson, in 1610. The term means "a wolf " or "wolves." This tribe must not be confounded with the Mohawks, who were of a different nation and language, or with the Mohegans of Connecticut, q. v.

Malecites or Marachites (Marechites), a branch of the Abnaki occupying the St. John river, New Brunswick. The term is said by Chamberlain to mean "broken-talkers." They were called "Armouchiquois" by the French Missionaries and their closest linguistic affinity is with the Passamaquoddy dialect. They are also known as "Maliseets."

Maquas. *Vide* Mohawks.

Marechites. *Vide* Malecites.

Mashpees or Marshpees, Wampanoags in and about the township of Mashpee, Barnstable Co., Mass. The name is derived from Indian words signifying "great pool." In 1660 Mashpee served as a reservation for the Christian Indians of the vicinity known as South Sea Indians. They intermarried with negroes freely and still later, with Hessians. In 1832 the mixed race numbered 332.

Massacos, a branch of the Tunxis, q. v. Known also as Simsburys, Conn.

Massachusetts, had dominion, for the most part over the eastern territory adjacent to Massachusetts Bay. The limitations of their territory, which was probably much more extensive, have not been accurately defined. About 1617 this tribe was decimated by a pestilence and their territory seems to have been divided amongst the Nipmucks, Narragansetts and other tribes. *Vide* Introduction.

Mattakees, a small tribe in Nauset territory (Mattakeset, Yarmouth, Barnstable Co., Mass.), probably subject to the Wampanoags. *Vide* Gookin, Mass. H. S. Col. 1st. Vol. 1, 148 (1806).

Micmacs. "The earliest aborigines of the American continent to to come in contact with Europeans." They constituted a large and influential tribe occupying mainly Nova Scotia, Prince

Edward's Island, Cape Breton, the northern part of New Brunswick and parts of Newfoundland. The French designated them as "Souriquois," and their name is supposed to signify "our allies." *Vide* Introduction.

Mohawks, the most eastern of "The Five Nations,"—Huron-Iroquois,—at one time, perhaps, the most powerful Indian confederacy that ever existed. The Mohawk villages occupied mainly the valleys of the Mohawk river. N. Y., and their name signifies "eaters of live meat"(*i. e.* bear). In the literature of New England they are designated by many names of which probably the most frequent are "Maquas" and "Mohocks."

Mohegans, a clan or division of the Pequots, fostered and ruled by Uncas after the death of Sassacus in 1637. Their original locality was on the Thames river, Conn., in the northern part of New London Co., but, as the results of subsequent conquests their territory became very much extended. The meaning of the name according to Trumbull, is "a wolf." *Vide* Introduction.

Montauks. This tribe formerly occupied the east end of Long Island, where they were at the head of thirteen tribes living there. They were closely related to the Indians of Massachusetts and of Connecticut. Although gradually decreasing, they preserved their hereditary chieftancy until 1875, when David Pharoah, their last king died.

Nashuas or Nashaways. These consisted of a tribe of Nipmucks who dwelt on or about the mouth of the Nashua river.

Naticks, a name applied to the Indians resident in and about the town of Natick in Middlesex, Mass. They belonged to the Mass: tribe and it was amongst them that the Rev. John Eliot established the first Indian Church in New England, in 1660. The meaning of the term is uncertain (Rider). *Vide* Mass. Place-Names.

Narragansets, a term derived from "the little island of Nahiganset" at the head of Point Judith Pond. (S. S. Rider.) *Vide Proper Names* in this volume. The territory occupied by this distinguished tribe, according to Gookin, extended about 30 or 40 miles from Sekunk and Narraganset Bay, including Rhode Island and other islands in that Bay. The Narragansets were separated from the Pequots by the Pawcatuck river. The most flourishing period in the history of this great tribe was in 1642 and under the chieftancy of Canonicus.

Nausets. This comparatively small tribe was located about the territory now known as Eastham in Plymouth Co. The Nausets appear to have been subject to the Wampanoags and they were the first tribe of Indians encountered by the Pilgrims after their arrival. (1620.)

Netops, these constituted a small tribe among the Sogkonates, q. v.

Newichewannocks. This tribe belonged to the Abnaki nation, and although their principal seat was on the Cocheco river, near Dover, N. H., they were intimately associated with the tribes occupying the Piscataqua river and its branches, Maine.

Niantics or Nehantics, these were really a tribe or branch of the Narragansets and resided principally at Wekapaug now Westerly in Rhode Island. Their chief sachem was Ninigret, a cousin of Miantunnomoh. A section of this tribe resided in Connecticut and were known as Western Niantics, q. v. The term means "At a point of land on a (tidal) river or estuary." J. H. T.

Nipmucks or Nipnets; this tribe dwelt mainly in the eastern interior of Massachusetts occupying many of the lakes and rivers. Their exact limits have not been defined but they must have been very extensive, as there is proof that their boundaries reached as far as Boston on the east, as far south as the northern portion of Rhode Island,—westward as far as Bennington in Vermont and as far north as Concord, New Hampshire. *Vide* Introduction.

Norridgewocks,—a branch of the Abnaki, who dwelt upon the Kennebec river.

Onagounges, a term applied by Mohawks to all the eastern Indians.

Pawtuckets, a branch of the Nipmucks, were located in Middlesex Co. on the territory now occupied by the town of Chelmsford, on the Merrimac river.

Passamaquoddies; this tribe was a branch of the Abnaki, being also known as Openangos. They were situated on the Schoodic river and on the waters and inlets of Passamaquoddy Bay, Me. The term means "pollock-plenty place."

Paugussetts, a tribe situated in and about Stratford, Huntington, and the surrounding townships in Connecticut. The territories of this clan stretched fifteen or eighteen miles along the coast and its number appears to have been very considerable. The Wepawaugs, who occupied the east bank of the Housatonic, opposite the Paugussetts, evidently belonged to the same people. *Vide* Wepawaugs.

Pennacooks: these formed part of the great Nipmuck confederacy occupying the banks of the Merrimack river in Massachusetts and New Hampshire under the valiant and judicious leadership of the great Passaconaway. The Pennacooks resided on the territory now occupied by the city of Concord, N. H., and the jurisdiction of Passaconaway extended at least, as far as Chelmsford, Middlesex Co., Mass., in a southerly direction, where the Pawtuckets were established.

Penobscots,—a branch of the Abnaki,—dwelt on an island in the Penobscot river, a few miles from Bangor, Maine.

Pequakets (Abnaki), occupied territory on the Saco river, especially about its sources, up to 1725, when they were exterminated by the English.

Pequots. This large and distinguished tribe was in all probability, originally descended from the Mahicans in New York State. Their territory extended from the Niantic river on the west to ten miles east of Paucatuck river, which divides Connecticut from Rhode Island (R. W.). Sassacus, their great sachem, had, it is said, no less than 26 sachems under him, when they were at their zenith. They were vanquished in 1637. *Vide* Introduction.

Podunks, a tribe occupying East Windsor and East Hartford, Conn. They appear to have been closely connected with the Poquonnuc Indians on the other side of the Connecticut river.

Pokanokets. *Vide* Wampanoags.

Potatucks, a Connecticut clan, who were located north-west of the Paugussetts, "within the limits of Newtown, Southbury, Woodbury, and some other townships," of whom little has been recorded, beyond the sales of their lands.

Quinnipiacs, the aboriginal inhabitants of New Haven, East Haven, Branford, and Guilford. Their territory extended from the Wepapaugs, on the west, to the Hammonassetts of Clinton and Killingworth, on the east. Their last sachem was said to have died about 1730. (De Forest.)

Ramapoos, a name by which the Ridgefield Indians of Conn. were known. They formed part of a tribe formerly existing at Greenwich, Stamford, and Norwalk and early in the 18th century they were ruled by a sachem named Catoonah. In 1708 they sold their lands and disbanded.

River Indians was a term applied to several tribes: thus the Mohicans or Mahicans dwelling south of the Iroquois, down the north side of the Hudson river, N. Y., were so denominated, as were also some clans of the Nipmucks, and, at an early period, all the Indians dwelling on the banks of the Connecticut River etc.

Rockomekos ("great corn-land") was the name of a tribe which constituted a branch of the Pequakets whose head-quarters were at Fryeburg, Me. They were exterminated by small-pox about the middle of the 18th century. Rockomeko was situated in the neighborhood of Canton, Oxford Co., Me.

Sokokis or Sockhigones, was the name of a branch of the Abnaki, settled on or about the Saco river, Me.

Souhegans, a branch of the New Hampshire Nipmucks, who lived upon the Souhegan river, and upon both banks of the Merrimack, above and below the mouth of the Souhegan.

Stockbridge or Housatonic Indians. These were located in Stockbridge ("Housatonic") Berkshire Co., Mass. and were principally known in connection with the missionary efforts made amongst them during many years, beginning from 1734. They subsequently removed to a town in Oneida Co., New York, after the Revolution, where they remained 34 years and still later, departed for Wisconsin.

Sogkonates, a tribe of which Awashonks was squaw-sachem. She exercised her sachemdom at or near the mouth of Seconnet river, and on the point then known as Sogkonate, later as Seconnet, and which now including the town of Little Compton, R. I., extends from Fogland ferry to the sea, in length between 7 and 8 miles. Here dwelt the Sogkonate tribe who, as far as can be judged, were numerous and who contributed to the downfall of Philip, although history contains few, if any, details of their achievements.

Tarratines or Tarrateens, a term used by Pilgrims and early settlers to denote the Abnaki; but while modern authorities seem inclined to accept this view there is doubt as to the aboriginal source of this term. After the exodus of the main body of the Abnaki to Canada the term Tarratines was applied to the Indians occupying the Penobscot river from source to sea and the contiguous territories.

Tunxis or Sepous, resided on the Farmington river, eight or ten miles west of the Connecticut. At an early period they were subject to Sequassen, the sachem who sold Hartford to the English, and they probably formed a part of the great confederacy which had formerly occupied the Connecticut valley.

Wabinga, a section of the Mahicans who were known also as River Indians. *Vide* River Indians. They had their dwellings "between the west branch of Delaware and Hudson's river, from Kittatinney ridge down to the ịriton." Jefferson's Notes, 308.

Wamesits were Nipmucks located near Wamesit Falls on the Concord river near its confluence with the Merrimack, in the neighborhood of the present city of Lowell, the site of which was the central point of the lands of the Pawtucket tribe. At Wamesit in 1674, there were 15 families of "Praying Indians", but a year or so later they were all disbanded or destroyed during Philip's war, and their lands were seized by their rapacious white conquerors.

Wampanoags or Pokanokets, the subjects of "Good Massassoit", and subsequently of his son, Philip, constituted the third greatest nation of the Indians in New England when it was settled by the English. The term has been defined by Dr. Trumbull, as meaning *Eastlanders,* and their territory included what is now called Bristol County (Rhode Island) Tiverton, Little Compton and the entire southern part of Plymouth Colony. The principal residence of the great chiefs of the Wampanoags was called Mount Hope, now included in Bristol, R. I. Pokanoket represented the dominion of the Wampanoags.

Wangunks, a Connecticut tribe of some importance, whose territories stretched from below Hartford to a considerable distance south of Middletown. Their chief sachem was named Sowheag.

Wawenocks, Waweenocks or Weweenocks constituted one of the main divisions of the Abnaki, and were said to be the immediate subjects of the great Bashaba or supreme ruler who resided in the vicinity of Pemaquid. Their settlement extended from the east of Sagadahoc to St. George river, but after the death of the Bashaba in 1615, they located on the west side of the Sheepscot river, near the lower falls. They were known as "the ancient regal race."

Wepawaugs; these lived on the eastern bank of the Housatonic river, Conn. and were probably identical with the Paugussetts, q. v.

Western Niantics, a sub-division of the Niantics, whose territory extended from Connecticut river eastward along the shore to Niantic river.

Zoquageers, a branch of the Abnaki who resided on the eastern shore of Lake Champlain.

Many other sub-ordinate tribes are mentioned in the early literature of New England, but they were comparatively unimportant.   The following list will serve as an example:—

Accominta, a small tribe formerly dwelling in a village named Agamenticus near the site of York, Maine.   They have been regarded as belonging to the Abnaki (Smith) but more probably as Pennacooks (Schoolcraft).   H-B. A-I. Vol. 1, p. 8.

Amaseconti or Aumissoukanti, an Abnaki tribe which occupied territory near Farmington Falls, Sandy River, Me.

Capawocks, Mass. Indians, settled at Martha's Vineyard.

Cushnocs, of Augusta, Me.; one of the Kanibas clans.

Manisses, the aborigines of Block Island, R. I.

Medoctee, a small Abnaki tribe, 1721, on St. John River, New Brunswick.

Missiassik, formerly living on Missisquoi River, Vermont, and probably "wanderers" related to Sokokis or Pequakki.

Muanbissik, unidentified, but mentioned as included among the Abnaki in a return sent to Governor of New England in 1721. H-B. of A-I. Vol. 1, p. 954.

Nawaas, an unidentified tribe dwelling between Scantic and Podunk, Conn.   A-I. H-B. Vol. 2, p. 46.

Pocomtocks, Mass. tribe, resident at Deerfield.

Quaboags, Nipmucks, in neighborhood of Brookfield, Mass.

Taconnets, of Waterville, Me.—a clan of the Norridgewocks.

Winnepesaukees, in the vicinity of Lake Winnepesaukee, N. H.

Wunnashowatuckoogs, a Nipmuck clan in Worcester Co., Mass. subject to Canonicus.

LIST OF ABNAKI WORDS*
(MAINE AND NEW HAMPSHIRE)

"The name Abnaki was first applied to the Indians in Nova Scotia, but was afterwards applied to all the tribes who resided east of the Massachusetts." (Crawford).

COMMON OBJECTS, ETC.

Awan, air;

Kzelomsen, wind;

Soglonbi, rain-water;

Nbisonbi, mineral-water;

Sobagw, sea or ocean;

Kchi alakws, morning or evening star;

Pili kisos, new moon;

Tka, cold;

Pekeda, smoke;

Siguana, last spring;

Nibena, last summer;

Pebona, last winter;

Nebi, water;

Pibganbi, muddy-water;

Skog, a serpent or snake;

Chegual, a frog;

Maska, a toad;

Wloda, heat;

*Selected from a Paper by the Hon. John G. Crawford, on "Indians of New Hampshire," in *Manchester Historic Collections*, Vol. I, part 2, 1898: by permission.

Kisos, sun, moon, month;
Skweda, fire, flame;
Siguan, spring;
Niben, summer;
Pebon, winter;
Taguogo, autumn;
Aremos (modern alemos,) a dog
Molsom, a wolf;
Wokwses, a fox;
Tmakwa, a beaver;
Nolka, a deer;
Nolkaüa, venison, or deer meat;
Magolibo, a caribou;
Pabigw, a flea;
Alikws, an ant;
Kemo, a louse;
Mamijola, a butterfly;
Mamaska, a toad
Skoks, a worm;
Sisikwa, a rattlesnake;
Mamselabika, a spider;
Wawilomwa, a bee;
Wjawas, a fly;
Pegues, a mosquito;

FOREST TREES, FRUIT, ETC.

Anaskemezi, an oak;
Wawabibagw, a poplar;
Manlakws, an ash;
Maskwamozi, a birch;
Kokokhoakw, a fir-tree;
Saskil, an elder;

Molodagw, a cedar;

Chignazakuam, a thorn-tree;

Maskwazimenakuam, a wild
   cherry-tree;

Senomozi, a maple;

Kanozas, a willow-tree;

Moskwaswaskw, the sweet flag;

Msoakw, a dry tree, decayed
   wood;

Maskwa, birch bark;

Pobnodageso, Tamarac;

Mskikoimins, a strawberry;
   (Plural *ak*)

Magoliboüa, caribou meat;

Magoliboawa, caribou skin;

Akigw, a seal;

Akigwawa, seal skin;

Nebes, a lake;

Nebesis, a pond;

Sen, a stone;

Pasaakw, a red-pine;

Masozial, ferns (*al* plural)

Asakuam, moss;

Walagaskw, bark;

Awazon, fuel, firewood;

Mskak, black spruce;

Sasogsek, sarsaparilla;

Anibi, an elm;

Wajoimizi, a beech;

Alnisedi, the hemlock;

Kawasen, a wind-fall;

Msazesso, white spruce;

Wdopi, an alder tree;

Wigkimizi, bass-wood;

Men or min, a berry;

Pessimen, currant (Plural *al*);

Awasos, a bear;

Anikwses, a striped squirrel;

A'sban, a racoon;

Agaskw, a woodchuck;

Sips, a bird;

Sibsis, a little bird;

Mgeso, an eagle;

Kokokhas, an owl

O'basas, a woodpecker;

Kwikueskas, a robin;

Senis, a pebble;

Pakesso, a partridge;

Mateguas, a rabbit;

Mikowa, a squirrel;

Wobikwsos, a mouse;

Moskuas, a musk-rat;

Mosbas, a mink;

Planigw, a flying squirrel;

Kogw, a porcupine;

Segogw, a skunk;

Mkazas, a crow;

Kchimkazas, a raven;

Kchi (great) makes raven 'the great crow'

Mkazawi, black (*ergo* crow);

Ahamo, a hen;

Ahamois, a chicken;

Nahama, a turkey;

Saguasis, a weasel;

FISH, ETC.

Namas, a fish;

Kabasa, a sturgeon;

Mskuamagw, a salmon;

Namagw, a salmon trout;

Kikomkwa, a sucker;

Nahoma, an eel;

Watagua, a pickerel;

Molazigan, a bass;

"Abazi, a tree, was not used in composition, but the termination, *akuam* was tree; thus Azawanimen, a plum, having the final *men*, is classed under the head of berry, and when applied to the tree became Azawanimenakuam, a plum-tree: Adbimen, a cherry, Adbimenakuam, a cherry-tree."

"The termination *mozi* signified a bush: squeskimenak, raspberries, squeskimenimozi, a raspberry bush:—sata, a blue-berry, satamozi, a blue-berry bush." (Crawford).

The mode of conjugating an Abnaki verb is also very interesting, as Mr. Crawford indicates. The letters N and K were used as personal pronouns, abbreviations representing the word *Nia*, I or me, and *Kia* thee or thou. In the plural N'was used for *Niuna*, us, we, when they did not include those to whom, and K,' *Kiuna* us, we, when those to whom they spoke were included; the apostrophe denoting the nasal sound. The following conjugation of the Indicative mood, Present tense, of the passive verb Kazalmegwzimuk, to be loved, will serve as an example:—

N'kezalmegwzi, I am loved.

'Kezalmegwzo, He is loved.

N'kezalmegwzibena, We are loved.

K'kezalmegwziba, You are loved.

'Kezalmegwzoak, They are loved.

W at the end of words is generally pronounced as oo, (double o) and, in other cases, when intended to be pronounced, is usually indicated by a special sign somewhat resembling an italic *w*.

BIBLIOGRAPHICAL LIST OF PRINCIPAL WORKS CONSULTED

History of New England.   Dr. Palfrey.

History of Massachusetts Bay.   Hutchinson, 2 vols., 1795.

History of Narraganset.   Hon. E. R. Potter.

History of Rhode Island.   Hon. S. G. Arnold.

History of Vermont.   Thompson.

History of Massachusetts.   G. L. Austin.

History of New England.   Governor Winthrop.

History of New Hampshire.   Belknap.

History of Maine, 2 vols.   Dr. Williamson.

Ancient Dominion of Maine.   Rufus King Sewall, 1859.

History of Vermont.   Dr. R. Williams, 2 vols, 1809.

Ogilby's "America," 1671.

"History of New York",   Broadhead.

"History of Indians of Connecticut."   De Forest, 1851.

Dr. A. Gallatin's "Vocabularies."

"Observations on Mohegan Language."   Jonathan Edwards.

"Biography and History of Indians of North America."   S. G. Drake, 1857.

Vocabulary of Mass. Indian Language.   Josiah Cotton.

Heckewelder's "On Indian Names."   Trans. Am. Philos. Soc. No. 4, 361.

"Indian Geographical Names," Trumbull; Conn. H. S. Col. Vol. 2, 1870.

"Indian Names of Places in Connecticut."   Dr. J. H. Trumbull.

"Indians of New Hampshire."   Hon. J. G. Crawford, 1898.

Gazateer of Massachusetts.   Elias Nason, 1874.

"Indian Names of Places in Rhode Island."   Dr. Usher Parsons, 1861.

"Key to the Indian Language."   Roger Williams; Mass. H. S. Co.

Church's "Indian Wars."   Edited by Drake, 1845.

"Early History of Vermont."   L. Wilbur, 1899.

History of Vermont.   Carpenter and Arthur, 1854.

History of Rhode Island.   Peterson, 1853.

History of Vermont.   Francis Chase.

Hayward's Gazateer of New Hampshire, 1849.

Farmer and Moore's Gazateer of New Hampshire, 1823.

"History of Manchester" (N. H.)   C. E. Potter, 1856.

"History of Hadley."   Judd.

"History of West Brookfield."   Temple.

Gazateer of Maine.   Varney.

"Woods and Lakes of Maine."   Lucius L. Hubbard, 1884.

Gazateer of Maine.   Hayward.

Natick Dictionary.   Dr. J. H. Trumbull.

"Indian Local Names."   S. G. Boyd, 1885.

Bartlett's Historical Records of Mass. and Conn.

"Historical Description of Boston."   Dr. Shurtleff.

"History and Antiquities of Boston."   Drake.

History of Andover, Mass.   Abiel Abbot, 1829.

"Historical Sketches of Andover," Mass.   Miss Bailey.

"Indian Names of Boston."etc.   E. N. Horsford, 1886.

"Indian Names in Salisbury, Conn."   J. W. Sanford, 1899.

Historical Sketch of Salisbury, Conn.   Malcolm S. Rudd, 1899.

"Bibliotheca Glottica."   Trübner, 1858.

"The Bibliography of Vermont."   Gilman, 1897.

Gazateer of Vermont.   Thompson.

"Indian Bulletin," for 1867.

Report of Am. Soc. for promoting the civilization of Indian tribes.   Greenleaf, 1823.

"Algic Researches." Schoolcraft, 1839.

Historical Gazateer of Vermont, Hemenway, 5 vols.

"Hand-book of the American Indians." Vol. I. and II. Bureau of Ethnology.

"The Lands of Rhode Island." Sidney S. Rider.

Pilling's "Bibliography of Algonquin Indians."

"Language of the Abnaquies." Willis.

"New England's Prospect." W. Wood, 1634.

"Bibliography of Local History of Mass." J. Colbourn.

"History of Augusta." J. W. North, 1870.

"History of Barrington." T. W. Bicknell, 1898.

"History of Westerly." Rev. F. Denison, 1878.

Place-Names of Providence Plantation (XVIIth century). Clarence S. Brigham, 1903.

"Names of Towns in Mass." W. H. Whitmore.

"History of Lynn." Newhall, 1865.

"Old Paths and Legends of New England." K. M. Abbott, 1903.

Johnston's Gazateer.

"On Plymouth Rock." S. Adams Drake, 1904.

Sketch of Dover, N. H. J. C. Stevens, 1833.

History of Concord, N. H. Nathaniel Bouton, 1856.

"Landmarks of Ancient Dover." Miss M. P. Thompson, 1892.

History of Concord, N. H. Edited by J. O. Lyford, 2 Vols. 1896.

"Purchas' Pilgrimage" (from Hakluyt Papers) 1628.

Reed's "History of Bath." 1894.

"Groton during the Indian Wars." Hon. S. A. Green, M.D., LL.D., 1883.

"Indian Deeds." H. A. Wright.

Mass. Bay Colonial Records.

Plymouth Records.

History of Derby. Orcutt.

Providence Early Records.

Registry of Deeds, Providence.

New Hampshire Records.

History of Waterbury.   Rev. Dr. Anderson.

Collected Records of Conn.

Conn. Records of Lands, etc.

Mass. Hist. Soc. Collections.

Mass. Hist. Soc. Proceedings.

Maine Hist. Soc. Collections.

Maine Register.

R. I. Historical Soc. Collections.

Numerous Encyclopædias, Maps, Deeds, Bulletins of Ethnological Bureau and of Geological Survey, many hundreds of Local Histories, etc., etc.

Also by R.A. Douglas-Lithgow:

NATIVE AMERICAN PLACE NAMES OF MASSACHUSETTS

NATIVE AMERICAN PLACE NAMES OF RHODE ISLAND

NATIVE AMERICAN PLACE NAMES OF CONNECTICUT

For more information about these and
other fine American reprints, contact

APPLEWOOD BOOKS
P.O. Box 365
Bedford, MA 01730